GCSE 9-1 ENGLISH LANGUAGE & LITERATURE AQA EXAM PRACTICE

Richard Durant

Author Richard Durant
English series editor Richard Durant
Editorial team Haremi Ltd
Series designers emc design ltd
Typesetting Newgen KnowledgeWorks (P) Ltd, Chennai, India
Illustrations Newgen KnowledgeWorks (P) Ltd, Chennai, India
App development Hannah Barnett, Phil Crothers and Haremi Ltd

Designed using Adobe InDesign
Published by Scholastic Education, an imprint of Scholastic Ltd, Book End, Range Road, Witney,
Oxfordshire, OX29 0YD
Registered office: Westfield Road, Southam, Warwickshire CV47 0RA
www.scholastic.co.uk

Printed and bound in India by Replika Press Pvt. Ltd.
© 2017 Scholastic Ltd
1 2 3 4 5 6 7 8 9   7 8 9 0 1 2 3 4 5 6

British Library Cataloguing-in-Publication Data
A catalogue record for this book is available from the British Library.
ISBN 978-1407-16915-6

Note from the publisher

Please use this product in conjunction with the official specifications for AQA GCSE 9–1 English
Language and AQA GCSE 9–1 English Literature and the sample assessment materials. Ask your teacher
if you are unsure where to find them.

The mark schemes in this book are simplified versions of the AQA GCSE 9–1 English Language and AQA
GCSE 9–1 English Literature mark schemes. See the AQA website for the official mark schemes.

Some answer space has been provided, but you will also need to use your own paper.

Practice papers for English Literature and the answers for the practice papers are available online.
Visit: www.scholastic.co.uk/gcse

Contents

Acknowledgements

The publishers gratefully acknowledge permission to reproduce the following copyright material:

Text permissions

pp.14, 15, 17: *Small Island*, Andrea Levy. Copyright © 2004 Andrea Levy. Reproduced by permission of Headline Publishing Group; p.42: Factory Media; p.43: *Travels with a Donkey in the Cevennes*, by Robert Louis Stevenson, 1879; pp.66, 68: *Macbeth*, William Shakespeare, Act 5 Scene 5, Cambridge School Shakespeare, Cambridge University Press; pp.73, 75: *A Christmas Carol*, Charles Dickens, Chapman & Hall, 1843; p.88: 'Mother, any distance greater than a single span', *Paper Aeroplane (Selected Poems)*, Simon Armitage, Faber and Faber Ltd; p.92: Your Dad Did What?, *Leaving and Leaving You*, Sophie Hannah, Carcanet Press, 1999, copyright Carcanet Press Limited, Manchester, UK, reprinted by kind permission; p.96: 'The Lesson' by Edward Lucie-Smith, from *101 Poems about Childhood*, ed. Michael Donaghy. Published by Faber & Faber, 2005. Copyright © Edward Lucie-Smith. Reproduced by permission of the author c/o Rogers, Coleridge & White Ltd., 20 Powis Mews, London, W11 1JN; pp.98, 99, 101: *A Clergyman's Daughter* by George Orwell (Copyright © George Orwell, 1935). Reprinted by permission of Bill Hamilton as the Literary Executor of the Estate of the Late Sonia Brownell; p.106: Durham Advertiser, 17 Feb 1882. Throughout: mark schemes adapted from AQA GCSE English Language 8700 and English Literature 8702, AQA 2016.

Photo permissions

p.28: Lisa S./Shutterstock.com; p.29: Angelo Giampiccolo/Shutterstock.com; p.33: Photo travel VlaD/Shutterstock.com; p.104: hraska/Shutterstock.com.

Every effort has been made to trace copyright holders for the works reproduced in this book, and the publishers apologise for any inadvertent omissions.

How to use this book

This Exam Practice Book has been produced to help you revise for your 9–1 GCSEs in AQA English Language and AQA English Literature. Written by an expert and packed full of helpful advice, preparation and exam-style questions, along with full practice papers, it will get you exam ready!

The best way to retain information is to take an active approach to revision. Don't just read the information you need to remember – do something with it! Transforming information from one form into another and applying your knowledge will ensure that it really sinks in. Throughout this book you'll find lots of features that will make your revision practice an active, successful process.

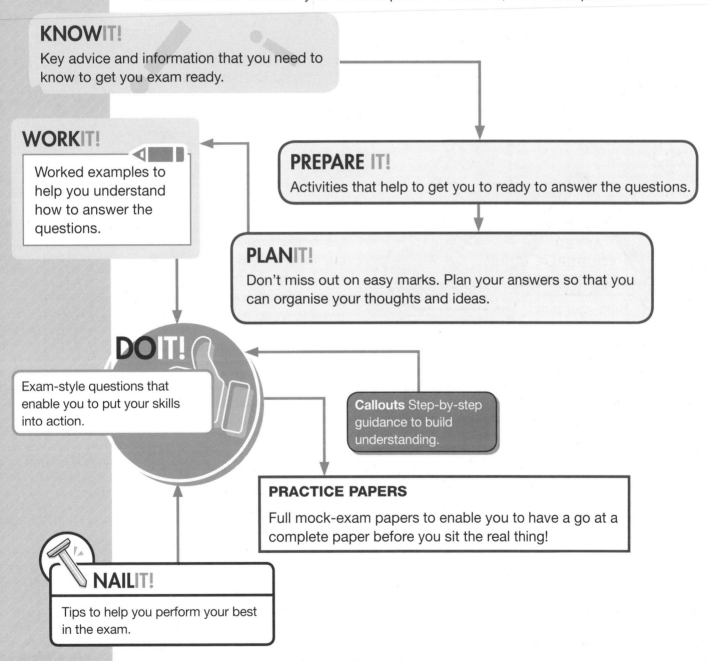

KNOWIT!
Key advice and information that you need to know to get you exam ready.

WORKIT!
Worked examples to help you understand how to answer the questions.

PREPARE IT!
Activities that help to get you to ready to answer the questions.

PLANIT!
Don't miss out on easy marks. Plan your answers so that you can organise your thoughts and ideas.

DOIT!
Exam-style questions that enable you to put your skills into action.

Callouts Step-by-step guidance to build understanding.

PRACTICE PAPERS
Full mock-exam papers to enable you to have a go at a complete paper before you sit the real thing!

NAILIT!
Tips to help you perform your best in the exam.

Use the AQA English Revision Guide alongside the Exam Practice Book for a complete revision and practice solution. Written by subject experts to match the new specification, the Revision Guide uses an active approach to revise all the content you need to know!

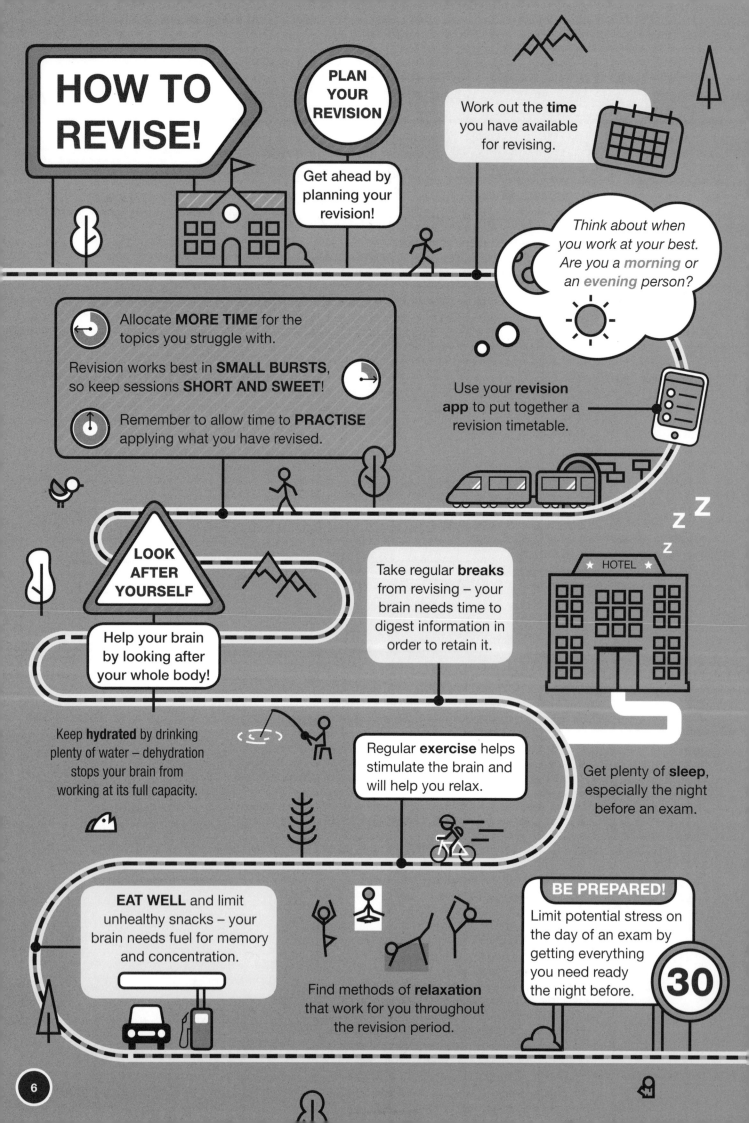

HOW TO REVISE!

PLAN YOUR REVISION

Get ahead by planning your revision!

Work out the **time** you have available for revising.

Think about when you work at your best. Are you a morning or an evening person?

Allocate **MORE TIME** for the topics you struggle with.

Revision works best in **SMALL BURSTS**, so keep sessions **SHORT AND SWEET**!

Remember to allow time to **PRACTISE** applying what you have revised.

Use your **revision app** to put together a revision timetable.

LOOK AFTER YOURSELF

Help your brain by looking after your whole body!

Take regular **breaks** from revising – your brain needs time to digest information in order to retain it.

★ HOTEL ★

Keep **hydrated** by drinking plenty of water – dehydration stops your brain from working at its full capacity.

Regular **exercise** helps stimulate the brain and will help you relax.

Get plenty of **sleep**, especially the night before an exam.

EAT WELL and limit unhealthy snacks – your brain needs fuel for memory and concentration.

Find methods of **relaxation** that work for you throughout the revision period.

BE PREPARED!

Limit potential stress on the day of an exam by getting everything you need ready the night before.

30

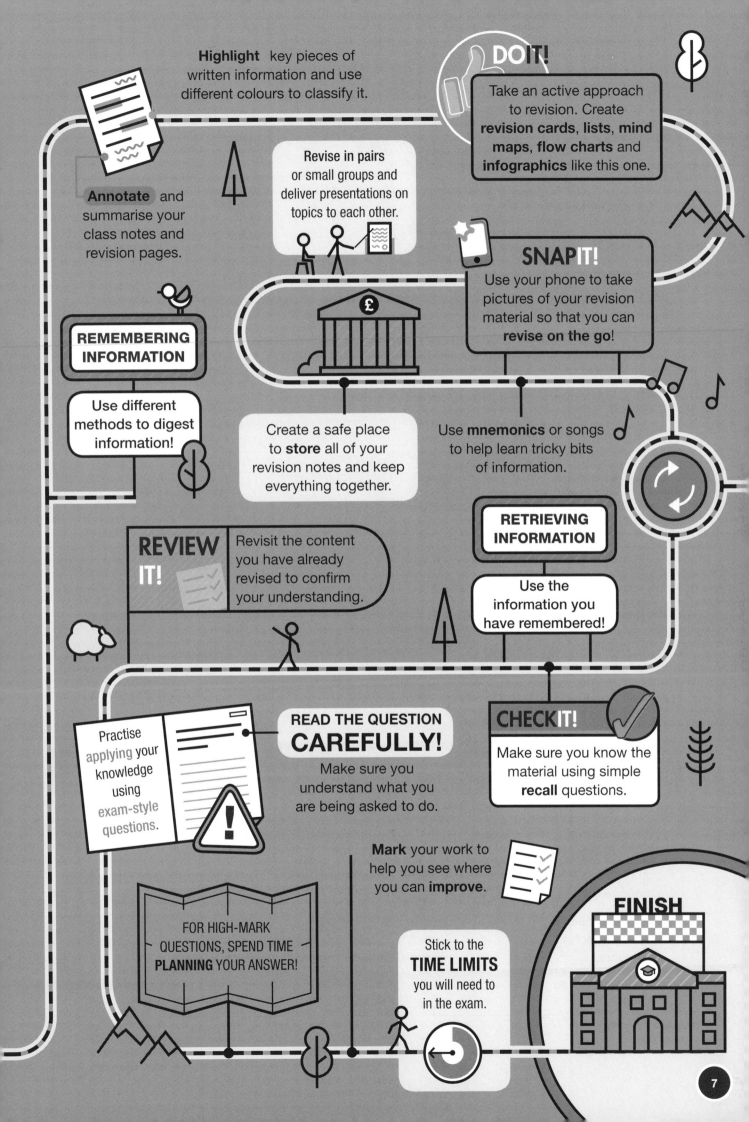

Highlight key pieces of written information and use different colours to classify it.

DO IT!
Take an active approach to revision. Create **revision cards**, **lists**, **mind maps**, **flow charts** and **infographics** like this one.

Annotate and summarise your class notes and revision pages.

Revise in pairs or small groups and deliver presentations on topics to each other.

SNAP IT!
Use your phone to take pictures of your revision material so that you can **revise on the go**!

REMEMBERING INFORMATION

Use different methods to digest information!

Create a safe place to **store** all of your revision notes and keep everything together.

Use **mnemonics** or songs to help learn tricky bits of information.

RETRIEVING INFORMATION

REVIEW IT! Revisit the content you have already revised to confirm your understanding.

Use the information you have remembered!

Practise **applying** your knowledge using **exam-style questions**.

READ THE QUESTION CAREFULLY!
Make sure you understand what you are being asked to do.

CHECK IT!
Make sure you know the material using simple **recall** questions.

Mark your work to help you see where you can **improve**.

FOR HIGH-MARK QUESTIONS, SPEND TIME **PLANNING** YOUR ANSWER!

Stick to the **TIME LIMITS** you will need to in the exam.

FINISH

ENGLISH LANGUAGE

KNOWIT!

There are two English Language papers:

☞ Paper 1: Explorations in creative reading and writing lasts 1 hour 45 minutes, and is worth 50 per cent of the GCSE.

☞ Paper 2: Writers' viewpoints and perspectives lasts 1 hour 45 minutes, and is worth 50 per cent of the GCSE.

This is how the English Language papers will be organised in the exam.

Exam	Section A: Reading	Section B: Writing
Paper 1: Explorations in creative reading and writing • 1 hour 45 minutes • 80 marks • 50% of GCSE	Answer four questions on part of a 20th/21st century literary fiction text. • 40 marks • 25% of GCSE	Write a description or a narrative (story). • 40 marks • 25% of GCSE
Paper 2: Writers' viewpoints and perspectives • 1 hour 45 minutes • 80 marks • 50% of GCSE	Answer four questions on two linked non-fiction texts. • 40 marks • 25% of GCSE	Write to present a viewpoint. • 40 marks • 25% of GCSE

When the examiners mark your answers, they refer to **mark schemes**. These mark schemes are made up of 'band descriptors'. Below are some simplified mark schemes for the two English Language papers. You will need to refer to these as you work through the book.

Paper 1 Section A: Reading

Question 2 mark scheme

Band 2 descriptors (Roughly GCSE grades 2–3)	Band 3 descriptors (Roughly GCSE grades 4–6)	Band 4 descriptors (Roughly GCSE grades 7–9)
The student's answer...	The student's answer...	The student's answer...
• shows some appreciation of language choices • comments on the effects of language choices • uses some relevant evidence, including quotations • tries to use some subject terminology.	• shows clear appreciation of language choices • explains the effects of some language choices • uses relevant evidence (including quotations) from different parts of the text • uses helpful, relevant subject terminology.	• examines language choices with insight and precision • closely analyses the effects of language choices • carefully chooses a variety of evidence, including quotations • uses a range of precise and helpful subject terminology.

Question 3 mark scheme

The mark scheme for Question 3 is similar to the mark scheme for Question 2, except that the focus is on **structural features** rather than **language choices**. The answer must give evidence – not necessarily quotations – and use subject terminology accurately.

Band 2 descriptors (Roughly GCSE grades 2–3)	Band 3 descriptors (Roughly GCSE grades 4–6)	Band 4 descriptors (Roughly GCSE grades 7–9)
The student's answer...	The student's answer...	The student's answer...
• shows some appreciation of structural features • comments on the effects of structural features • uses some relevant evidence • tries to use some subject terminology.	• shows clear appreciation of relevant structural features • explains the effects of some relevant structural features • uses different forms of relevant evidence • uses helpful, relevant subject terminology.	• examines relevant structural features with insight and precision • closely analyses the effects of relevant structural features • carefully chooses a variety of evidence • uses a range of precise and helpful subject terminology.

Question 4 mark scheme

Here are the sort of descriptors that exam markers will use when they mark Question 4.

Band 2 descriptors (Roughly GCSE grades 2–3)	Band 3 descriptors (Roughly GCSE grades 4–6)	Band 4 descriptors (Roughly GCSE grades 7–9)
The student's answer...	The student's answer...	The student's answer...
• tries to make some comments that evaluate the text • refers to a relevant example from the text • refers to some of the writer's techniques • uses a couple of helpful quotations.	• includes a clear evaluation • gives examples that support and clarify points • helpfully explains the effects of some of the writer's techniques • uses helpful quotations from different parts of the text.	• critically evaluates the text in a detailed way • gives examples from the text to explain views convincingly • analyses effects of a range of the writer's choices • justifies points with relevant quotations from different parts of the text.

Paper 1 Section B: Writing

Whatever category the writing task belongs to, it is meant to help you to write creatively. The skills required by the task are always the same, and every task will be marked against the same mark scheme.

Here are the sort of descriptors that exam markers will use when they mark your writing.

Band 2 descriptors (Roughly GCSE grades 2–3)	Band 3 descriptors (Roughly GCSE grades 4–6)	Band 4 descriptors (Roughly GCSE grades 7–9)
Content The student's answer…	**Content** The student's answer…	**Content** The student's answer…
• is mainly clear in expression • keeps trying to match register to purpose, form and audience • chooses words with some care • uses some linguistic devices.	• is clear, effective and engaging throughout • mainly matches register to purpose, form and audience • precisely chooses words and phrases for deliberate effect • uses varied linguistic devices for impact.	• wins the reader over and holds their interest throughout • precisely matches register to purpose, form and audience • uses a wide and adventurous vocabulary • carefully chooses linguistic devices for effect throughout.
Organisation The student's answer…	**Organisation** The student's answer…	**Organisation** The student's answer…
• uses suitable ideas that have some variety and sometimes link together • uses some paragraphs and discourse markers • uses some other structural features (for example, deliberate repetition, topic sentences).	• uses varied ideas, linking them well • carefully organises paragraphs around well-chosen discourse markers • uses structural features for deliberate impact.	• is highly structured and developed around a range of dynamic and complex ideas • is highly coherent and fluent in organisation, incorporating discourse markers in a natural way • uses a range of structural features skilfully and creatively.

Paper 2 Section A: Reading

Question 2 mark scheme

Band 2 descriptors (Roughly GCSE grades 2–3)	Band 3 descriptors (Roughly GCSE grades 4–6)	Band 4 descriptors (Roughly GCSE grades 7–9)
The student writes about...	The student writes about...	The student writes about...
... at least one of the texts, and: • interprets • tries to infer • chooses some appropriate detail • points out some relevant similarities and/or difference(s).	... both texts, and: • clearly synthesises and interprets • makes clear inferences • chooses clear, relevant details • points out clear, relevant similarities and/or differences between texts.	... both texts, and: • perceptively synthesises and interprets • makes perceptive inferences • chooses very precise, relevant details • explores perceptive, relevant similarities and/or differences between texts.

Question 3 mark scheme

Band 2 descriptors (Roughly GCSE grades 2–3)	Band 3 descriptors (Roughly GCSE grades 4–6)	Band 4 descriptors (Roughly GCSE grades 7–9)
The student's answer...	The student's answer...	The student's answer...
• shows some understanding of language • attempts to comment on the effect of language • uses some appropriate textual detail • makes some use of subject terminology, mainly appropriately.	• shows clear understanding of language • explains clearly the effects of the writer's choices of language • uses a range of relevant textual detail • makes clear and accurate use of subject terminology.	• shows clear understanding of language • explains clearly the effects of the writer's choices of language • uses a range of relevant textual detail • makes clear and accurate use of subject terminology.

Question 4 mark scheme

Band 2 descriptors (Roughly GCSE grades 2–3)	Band 3 descriptors (Roughly GCSE grades 4–6)	Band 4 descriptors (Roughly GCSE grades 7–9)
The student's answer...	The student's answer...	The student's answer...
• tries to compare ideas and perspectives • makes some comments on how writers' methods are used • chooses some appropriate textual detail/references, not always supporting from one or both texts • identifies some different ideas and perspectives.	• compares ideas and perspectives in a clear and relevant way • explains clearly how writers' methods are used • selects relevant detail to support from both texts • shows a clear understanding of the different ideas and perspectives in both texts.	• compares ideas and perspectives in a perceptive way • analyses how writers' methods are used • selects a range of judicious supporting detail from both texts • shows a detailed understanding of the different ideas and perspectives in both texts.

Paper 2 Section B: Writing

The mark scheme for Paper 2 Section B: Writing is the same as the mark scheme for Paper 1 Section B: Writing on page 10.

Technical accuracy

The mark scheme for technical accuracy is the same for the writing tasks in both English Language papers. (There are no technical accuracy marks to be won or lost when you are answering the reading questions.)

Aspect	Band 2 descriptors (Roughly GCSE grades 2–3)	Band 3 descriptors (Roughly GCSE grades 4–6)	Band 4 descriptors (Roughly GCSE grades 7–9)
	The student's answer…	The student's answer…	The student's answer…
Sentence demarcation	• marks the beginnings and ends of most sentences	• marks the beginnings and ends of almost all sentences	• correctly marks the beginnings and ends of sentences
Punctuation	• often uses basic punctuation well	• uses a range of punctuation usually correctly	• uses a wide range of punctuation almost always correctly
Sentences	• tries out different sentence structures and types	• varies sentences for effect	• uses a wide range of sentence structures confidently and effectively
Standard English	• sometimes uses Standard English, perhaps with some mistakes over agreement or tense endings	• mainly uses Standard English with good control and flexibility	• uses appropriate Standard English with control and flexibility throughout
Spelling	• sometimes spells more complex words correctly (such as, height, definite)	• makes few spelling mistakes – even complex and irregular words (such as accommodation, rhythmic, parallel)	• spells almost all words correctly, including adventurous vocabulary (such as combustible, opprobrium, machination)
Vocabulary	• varies vocabulary.	• chooses some precise and sophisticated vocabulary.	• uses a wide and adventurous vocabulary.

Paper 1 Section A: Reading
Introduction and advice

KNOWIT!

There are two sections in Paper 1. Section A: Reading comes first. Here is a rough guide to how you should allocate your time:

☞ Spend 15 minutes reading the fiction text.

☞ Spend 40 minutes answering the four questions.

☞ Leave 5 minutes at the end to check your answers.

The questions have different focuses and are worth different amounts of marks. Here are the focuses, mark allocations and how long you should spend answering each question:

☞ Question 1: identifying information at the start of the text (4 marks/4 minutes).

☞ Question 2: the effects of the writer's language choices (8 marks/8 minutes).

☞ Question 3: the effects of how the writer structures the text (8 marks/8 minutes).

☞ Question 4: evaluation of the text and its impact on a reader (20 marks/20 minutes).

Here is the sort of text you will get in Paper 1:

Source A
This extract is from early in a novel by Andrea Levy. In this section, Hortense has arrived in London to join her husband after a long journey by sea from Jamaica. She arrives at the address her husband has given her.

Small Island

The door was answered by an Englishwoman. A blonde-haired, pink-cheeked Englishwoman with eyes so blue they were the brightest thing in the street. She looked on my face, parted her slender lips and said, 'Yes?'

5 'Is this the household of Mr Gilbert Joseph?'

'I beg your pardon?'

'Gilbert Joseph?' I said, a little slower.

'Oh, Gilbert. Who are you?' She pronounced Gilbert so strangely that for a moment I was anxious that I would be delivered to 10 the wrong man.

'Mr Gilbert Joseph is my husband – I am his wife.'

The woman's face looked puzzled and pleased all at one time. She looked back into the house, lifting her head as she did. Then she turned to me and said, 'Didn't he come to meet you?'

15 'I have not seen Gilbert,' I told her, then went on to ask, 'but this is perchance where he is aboding?'

At which this Englishwoman said, 'What?' She frowned and looked over my shoulder at the trunk, which was resting by the kerbside where it had been placed by the driver of the taxi
20 vehicle. 'Is that yours?' she enquired.

'It is.'

'It's the size of the Isle of Wight. How did you get it here?' She laughed a little. A gentle giggle that played round her eyes and mouth.

25 I laughed too, so as not to give her the notion that I did not know what she was talking about as regards this 'white island'. I said, 'I came in a taxicab and the driver assured me that this was the right address. Is this the house of Gilbert Joseph?'

The woman stood for a little while before answering by saying,
30 'Hang on here. I'll see if he's in his room.' She then shut the door in my face.

And I wondered how could a person only five feet six inches tall (five feet seven if I was wearing my wedding-shoe heels), how could such a person get to the top of this tall house? Ropes
35 and pulleys was all I could conceive. Ropes and pulleys to hoist me up. We had stairs in Jamaica. Even in our single-storey houses we had stairs that lifted visitors on to the veranda and another that took them into the kitchen. There were stairs at my college, up to the dormitories that housed the pupils on
40 two separate floors. I was very familiar with stairs. But all my mind could conjure as I looked up at this tall, tall house was ropes and pulleys. It was obvious that I had been on a ship for too long.

You will need to refer to this extract when you look at the pages that follow on **questions 1–4**.

KNOWIT!

☞ Question 1 will always ask you to find some **information**. The exam marker wants to know if you can find information that is either right there in front of you, or needs a small amount of working out or inferring.

☞ You should spend 4 minutes on this question.

☞ It is worth 4 marks.

Here is an example Question 1:

> Read again the first part of the Source from **lines 1 to 7**.
>
> List **four** facts from this part of the text about the Englishwoman's appearance.
>
> **[4 marks]**

PREPAREIT!

Before you attempt to answer the question, it is important that you understand what the question is asking you to do. You should 'prepare' the question by underlining the key words and annotating it with your initial thoughts and ideas.

Mark up the question above and re-read lines 1 to 7. Add some notes to the extract on page 14.

DO IT!

Now answer the question you have just prepared in the space below.

1 ....

....

2 ....

....

3 ....

....

4 ....

....

Question 2

KNOWIT!

☞ Question 2 will always be about the writer's **language choices** and the **effect** of these language choices on the reader.

☞ You should spend 8 minutes on this question.

☞ It is worth 8 marks.

Here is an example Question 2:

Look in detail at this extract from **lines 15 to 31** of the Source:

15   'I have not seen Gilbert,' I told her, then went on to ask, 'but this is perchance where he is aboding?'

At which this Englishwoman said, 'What?' She frowned and looked over my shoulder at the trunk, which was resting by the kerbside where it had been placed by the driver of the taxi
20   vehicle. 'Is that yours?' she enquired.

'It is.'

'It's the size of the Isle of Wight. How did you get it here?' She laughed a little. A gentle giggle that played round her eyes and mouth.

25   I laughed too, so as not to give her the notion that I did not know what she was talking about as regards this 'white island'. I said, 'I came in a taxicab and the driver assured me that this was the right address. Is this the house of Gilbert Joseph?'

The woman stood for a little while before answering by saying,
30   'Hang on here. I'll see if he's in his room.' She then shut the door in my face.

How does the writer use language here to suggest how Hortense and the Englishwoman misunderstand each other?

You could include the writer's choice of:

• words and phrases

• language features and techniques

• sentence forms.

[8 marks]

PREPAREIT!

Prepare to answer the question by underlining the key words in the question and annotating it with your initial thoughts and ideas. Mark up the extract with the question in mind.

WORKIT!

Here is the first half of a student's answer to the question on page 17:

> Everything about the choice of language emphasises the two women's misunderstanding of each other. Presumably, Hortense feels intimidated by the Englishwoman and so she tries to use very impressive words - 'perchance' and 'aboding'. However, Hortense does not realise that the Englishwoman is a very ordinary person - not posh at all - who will not understand complex words. The woman's ordinariness is clearly signalled to the reader by her response with the direct, even rude question, 'What?'. There is a cultural misunderstanding between the two women which comes across in the form of language. For example, when the woman makes a joke about Hortense's luggage being as large as the Isle of Wight, Hortense takes this as meaning a 'white island'.

Use the mark scheme for Question 2 on page 8 to write the second half of this student's answer. Comment on the sorts of sentences the writer uses, and the effect this has on her description of the scene.

The writer has used simple sentences to…

....

....

....

....

....

....

....

....

....

....

....

....

....

....

....

....

....

....

DO IT!

Here are two more example questions for you to answer. They both use the extract on page 17. Use the space provided to write your answer and continue on your own paper.

How does the writer use language here to show the two women's thoughts and feelings?

You could include the writer's choice of:

- words and phrases

- language features and techniques

- sentence forms.

[8 marks]

....

....

....

....

....

....

....

....

....

....

....

....

....

....

....

....

....

....

....

....

DO IT!

How does the writer use language here to create a contrast between the two women?

You could include the writer's choice of:

- words and phrases
- language features and techniques
- sentence forms.

[8 marks]

....

....

....

....

....

....

....

....

....

....

....

....

....

....

....

....

....

....

....

....

....

Question 3

KNOWIT!

☞ Question 3 will always be about how the writer has **structured** (organised) the whole extract to have an **effect** on the reader.

☞ You will need to use relevant subject terminology to support your views.

☞ You should spend 8 minutes on this question.

☞ It is worth 8 marks.

Here is a example Question 3:

You now need to think about the **whole** of the **Source**.

This text represents a dramatic and amusing episode early in the novel.

How has the writer structured the text to interest you as a reader?

You could write about:

• what the writer focuses your attention on at the beginning

• how and why the writer changes this focus as the Source develops

• any other structural features that interest you.

[8 marks]

PREPAREIT!

Prepare the question by underlining the key words and annotating it with your initial thoughts and ideas. Mark up the extract on pages 14–15 with the question in mind.

WORKIT!

Below is what one student wrote for the example Question 3 you were shown on page 21. The exam marker has made a few comments in the margin:

> This opening has a strong impact. The Englishwoman who opens the door is so simply described that we can 'see' her face in our minds straight away and we are intrigued by who she might be. (Although we might know her well if we had read the whole novel.) The first paragraph contains a strong piece of characterisation - a woman who is very self-confident and perhaps direct and impatient. It is as though we have been delivered straight into the scene and we are standing on the doorstep with Hortense. The next few lines are dialogue between the two women, and this keeps us - the reader - 'in the moment'. We are not being given narrative to explain the situation and we seem to share the astonishment of the two women. Our confusion keeps growing with the women's puzzlement: What does the woman mean by 'I beg your pardon' - is she puzzled, offended, aggressive perhaps? We are left wondering what the relationship between these two women could be - especially as one seems to be living with the other one's husband!
>
> The next section is based around a series of misunderstandings - the two women are using mismatching language, and the joke that one of them makes is completely misunderstood by the other - possibly as a racist attack on her (assuming she is a black Jamaican). The final part of the source changes from dialogue and confusion to one character thinking about her situation, and this attempt to make sense of her feelings and her circumstances is sort of shared by the reader. At the very end of the source the narrator comes to a sort of interim conclusion: perhaps she was disorientated by her long voyage when she was living on a ship.

Margin comments:
- Opening/intriguing reader
- Subject terminology
- Dialogue as structural feature
- Unfolding detail
- Leading the reader through the text via their curiosity
- Commentary/ conclusion

This is what an exam marker says about the student's answer:

> This answer shows a clear understanding of a number of structural features – opening, how detail is provided gradually to inform and intrigue and the use of dialogue. Some of this is perceptive, but mainly features are described and explained, without their effects being analysed. This would have involved exploring the use and effects of at least one main structural feature. There is a good attention to details and some specific examples are mentioned to support points. Terminology used is helpful (characterisation, paragraph, dialogue) but often quite limited. Terminology could have been more precise (e.g. 'language register'). This answer is in the upper half of Band 3.

Use the exam marker's comments and the mark scheme on page 9 to rewrite the student's answer in order to improve it. Use the space below and then continue on your own paper.

....

....

....

....

....

DO IT!

Now have a go at the question below. Use the space provided to write your answer and continue on your own paper if necessary.

You need to think about the **whole** of the **Source**.

This text is from early in the novel. How has the writer structured the text to suggest the conflicts and confusion in Hortense's mind? You could write about:

- what the writer focuses your attention on at the beginning
- how and why the writer changes this focus as the Source develops
- any other structural features that interest you.

[8 marks]

Question 4

Here is an example Question 4:

Focus this part of your answer on the second part of the Source from **line 17 to the end**.

When the book was published, a critic said: 'At this point in the novel the reader gets a very clear sense of Hortense's personality and her values.'

To what extent do you agree?

In your response, you could:

• consider your own impressions of Hortense in this part of the novel

• evaluate how the writer creates the reader's response to Hortense

• support your opinions with references to the text.

[20 marks]

PLANIT!

Look at the question that you prepared on your sense of Hortense's personality and her values. Make a quick plan for your answer.

PLANIT!

DOIT!

Write your answer to Question 4 you have been preparing and planning (on pages 24 and 25) about your sense of Hortense's personality and her values.

....

....

....

....

....

....

....

....

....

....

....

....

....

....

....

....

....

....

....

....

....

....

....

....

....

DO IT!

Here is another Question 4 for you to answer. Use the space below to answer the question and continue on your own paper if necessary.

Focus this part of your answer on the second part of the Source from **line 15 to the end**.

One reader, having read this section of the text said: 'Even though Hortense makes obvious mistakes that make her look foolish, we find ourselves warming to her.'

To what extent do you agree?

In your response, you could:

- consider your own impressions of Hortense

- evaluate how the writer conveys Hortense's thoughts and feelings

- support your opinions with references to the text.

[20 marks]

Paper 1 Section B: Writing
Introduction and advice

KNOWIT!

☞ Question 5 of Paper 1 Section B: Writing will ask you to write **creatively**, inspired by a topic linked to the texts in the reading section of Paper 1.

☞ There will only be two tasks and you must choose **one** of them.

☞ You should spend 45 minutes on the planning and writing.

☞ There are 40 marks for the writing task.

  • 24 of the marks are for content – your ideas and information and organisation – how you organise the content

  • 16 of the marks are for technical accuracy – spelling, punctuation and grammar.

☞ The question (the task) will give you a context for your writing: an audience (reader), purpose and form. This context will apply to both writing tasks. The purpose will be to describe or to narrate.

☞ The stimulus for one of the two questions will be a picture.

NAILIT!

Spend 45 minutes on planning, writing and checking your work:

• 5 minutes preparing and planning
• 35 minutes writing
• 5 minutes checking and correcting

There are five possible sorts of task that can be set on this paper:

Question type 1: descriptive writing with a visual stimulus

> An environmental organisation is planning a booklet of writing by young people under the title: 'When nature hits back'.
>
> Entries for the booklet will be chosen by four senior civil servants in the government's Environment Agency.
>
> Write a description suggested by the picture.

Question type 2: descriptive writing without a visual stimulus

> Describe an occasion when you had to make a difficult decision.
>
> Focus on the thoughts and feelings you had at that time.

Question type 3: narrative with a visual stimulus

> Write a story set during a flood as suggested by the picture.

Question type 4: narrative – writing the opening to a story

> Write the opening part of a story about an unusual journey.

Question type 5: narrative – writing a complete story

> Write a story about a misunderstanding.

Question type 1: descriptive writing with a visual stimulus

Here is an example question:

A charity is running a creative writing competition under the title: 'Street life'.

Entries for the competition will be judged by a panel of leaders of large companies.

Write a description suggested by this picture:

(24 marks for content and organisation
16 marks for technical accuracy)
[40 marks]

PREPAREIT!

Prepare the question by underlining the key words and annotating it with your initial thoughts and ideas. Annotate the image with some notes about what you can see.

PLANIT!

Use the four boxes below to plan your answer.

Paragraph 1:

Paragraph 2:

Paragraph 3:

Paragraph 4:

DOIT!

Use the space below to write an opening paragraph for the 'Street life' competition task. Then use your own paper to write the rest of your description.

....

....

....

....

....

....

DOIT!

Now have a go at answering the *descriptive writing with a visual stimulus* question on page 28. Use your own paper to prepare and plan your answer as you have done above.

Question type 2: descriptive writing without a visual stimulus

Here is an example question:

Describe an occasion when something exciting happened. Focus on the thoughts and feelings you had at that time.

(24 marks for content and organisation
16 marks for technical accuracy)

[40 marks]

PREPAREIT!

Underline the key words in the question, so that you are sure what the question is asking you to do. Jot down some of your first thoughts and ideas.

NAILIT!

Make sure you **describe**. Don't just tell a story.

PLANIT!

Use the four boxes below to plan your answer. A few ideas on how to organise the question have been suggested, but you don't have to use them.

Paragraph 1: anticipation of the event or what life was like before if the event was unexpected. Describe mood, feelings.

Paragraph 2: start of event. Describe details, especially sights, sounds, and so on.

Paragraph 3: during the event/event develops.

Paragraph 4: after the event/results of the event. Feelings now.

DO IT!

Use the space below to answer the question. Continue on your own paper.

DO IT!

Now have a go at answering the *descriptive writing without a visual stimulus* question on page 28. Use your own paper to prepare, plan and answer your question.

NAILIT!

Check through your writing. Make sure you have:

- used an appropriate style, tone and vocabulary
- not made any careless mistakes.

Question type 3: narrative with a visual stimulus

Here is an example question:

You are going to enter a creative writing competition.

Your entry will be judged by a panel of people of your own age.

Write a story suggested by this picture:

(24 marks for content and organisation
16 marks for technical accuracy)
[40 marks]

PREPAREIT!

Prepare the question by underlining the key words and annotating it with your initial thoughts and ideas. Annotate the image with some notes about what you can see.

PLANIT!

Use the boxes below to gather your thoughts and ideas and plan your answer.

NAILIT!

Before you write the opener to your story, you should ask yourself the following questions:

- How can I use language that is clear and creative?
- How will I engage my reader straight away?

DOIT!

Write the opening of the story in the space provided.

DO IT!

Use the space below to continue your story suggested by the balloon picture. Continue on your own paper if necessary.

....

....

....

....

....

....

....

....

....

....

....

....

....

....

....

....

....

....

....

....

....

DO IT!

Now have a go at answering the *narrative with a visual stimulus* question on page 28. Use your own paper to prepare, plan and answer your question.

Question type 4: narrative – writing the opening to a story

Here is an example question:

> Write the opening of a story called 'Getting away'.
>
> (24 marks for content and organisation
> 16 marks for technical accuracy)
> **[40 marks]**

PREPAREIT!

Prepare the question by underlining the key words and annotating it with your initial thoughts and ideas.

WORKIT!

Here is the beginning of one student's opening to their 'Getting away' story:

> At last Tessa was ready. The oars were neatly stacked in the boat along with all the water and food and equipment and everything she might need on her journey. She pushed hard and finally the boat began to scrunch along the sand until it got into the water. She could feel her injured arm aching with every movement, but she pushed and pushed until the boat was floating about. Now she felt a lot of joy because she was getting away. Suddenly her enthusiasm changed to worry because of how long would she be on her own on the sea? Could she survive long enough? She didn't know.

Look at the mark scheme on page 10. Decide whether the writing currently fits most closely into Band 2 or Band 3. Now rewrite the beginning of the opening so that you improve it. Use the mark scheme descriptors to guide your improvements.

....

....

....

....

....

....

....

....

....

....

....

PLANIT!

Plan your own opening of a story called 'Getting away' in the space below.

DOIT!

Write the opening of your story called 'Getting away' in the space provided and continue on your own paper.

DO IT!

Now try this question using the space below. Continue on your own paper if necessary. Remember to prepare and plan!

An accident prevention charity is planning to publish a series of stories about risks for children during school holidays. You have been invited to do some creative writing for the series.

Write the opening of a story called 'The dare'.

(24 marks for content and organisation
16 marks for technical accuracy)
[40 marks]

DO IT!

Have a go at answering the *narrative – writing the opening to a story* question on page 28. Use your own paper to prepare, plan and answer your question.

Question type 5: narrative – writing a complete story

Here is an example question:

> You have been invited to produce a piece of creative writing set in one place.
>
> Write a story about something that happens in an empty building.
>
> (24 marks for content and organisation
> 16 marks for technical accuracy)
> **[40 marks]**

PREPAREIT!

Underline the key words in the question, so that you are sure what the question is asking you to do. Jot down some of your first thoughts and ideas.

WORKIT!

Here is part of one student's answer. Notice how the student is trying to develop the story at this point.

> ... became less confident. His behaviour became less joky and carefree. He too was beginning to think about what might happen next.
>
> Omran had lost his confidence long ago. He hated cobwebs and dark, damp places, but he pushed on until he could no longer hear the others wimpering and whining. He could not see anything now and so he held out his hands and tried to feel what was ahead. He stumbled occasionally as he went forward and he had to reach out to find something to help him keep his balance so that he wouldn't just fall flat on his face into something nasty. Then he reached something solid that he couldn't get past.

Look at the mark scheme on page 10. Decide whether the writing currently fits most closely into Band 2 or Band 3. Rewrite this part of the story so that you improve it in the space provided below. Use the mark scheme descriptors to guide your improvements.

....

....

....

....

....

....

....

Write the rest of the 'empty building' story on a separate piece of paper.

DO IT!

Now try this question. Remember to prepare and plan! Use the space below and continue on your own paper if necessary.

> You are going to enter a creative writing competition.
>
> Your entry will be judged by a panel of people of your own age.
>
> Write a story about two teenagers who get lost together.
>
> (24 marks for content and organisation
> 16 marks for technical accuracy)
> **[40 marks]**

DO IT!

Have a go at answering the *narrative – writing a complete story* question on page 28. Use your own paper to prepare, plan and answer your question.

Paper 2 Section A: Reading
Introduction and advice

KNOWIT!

There are two sections in Paper 2. Section A: Reading comes first.

You will be given two linked sources from different time periods and genres in order to consider how each presents a perspective or viewpoint to influence the reader. The sources will be non-fiction and literary non-fiction texts. They will be drawn from the 19th century, and either the 20th or 21st century. The texts may include:

☞ articles

☞ reports

☞ essays

☞ articles

☞ letters

☞ diaries.

Here is a rough guide to how you should allocate your time:

☞ Spend 15 minutes reading the two texts and the four questions you are given.

☞ Spend 40 minutes answering the four questions.

☞ Leave 5 minutes at the end to check your answers.

The questions have different focuses and are worth different amounts of marks. Here are the focuses, mark allocations and how long you should spend answering each question:

☞ Question 1: identify and interpret explicit and implicit information and ideas (4 marks/4 minutes).

☞ Question 2: select and synthesise evidence from different texts (8 marks/8 minutes).

☞ Question 3: how writers use language to achieve effects and influence readers (12 marks/12 minutes).

☞ Question 4: compare writers' ideas and perspectives, and how these are conveyed (16 marks/16 minutes).

On pages 42 and 43 are examples of the sorts of text you will get in Paper 2 Section A.

Source A – 21st century non-fiction

From 'A beginner's guide to wild camping gear'

Wild camping will obviously mean carrying everything you need with you, so with everything you take, consider the weight.

You'll be needing:

Shelter: Most likely a tent, but that's not the end of the story.

5 **Sleeping bag and mat**: Your bed for the night: do not underestimate the importance of a good night's sleep!

Food, drink & some way of cooking it: You need fuel for your body and fuel to cook it with. We'll check out a few different approaches.

Clothing: General outdoor wear, naturally, but we'll examine how to
10 give it a wild camping slant.

Rucksack: Simply put – big enough but not too big; comfortable to carry.

A few choice extras to make it all more comfortable.

Let's start with shelter…

Tent

15 You'll notice we said 'shelter' just then. Well, by and large, this will mean a tent, but there are other options. In fact, those other options would be regarded by some as the very essence of wild camping, but we'll come to those ideas later.

If you're intending to wild camp, you should try to avoid brightly
20 coloured tents. That needn't mean obsessively searching out something with a camo-print flysheet, but if you're trying to blend in discreetly and not be noticed, vibrant orange isn't very sensible.

The 'best' tent is the one which offers the best trade-off between comfort when you're in it and comfort when you're carrying it. Where that balance
25 should be struck is different for everyone, so you'll have to make that judgement for yourself. Bear in mind though, this is not really a luxury activity, and you're likely to be somewhere remote… which means carrying it a fair old way. You don't want to be cursing the weight on your back with every overloaded step you take. Most of your time inside the
30 tent will be spent sleeping, most of the time carrying it you'll be awake! For that reason, for the sake of being unobtrusive, and because big tents don't fit easily into small spaces, small and light is a good bet…

Other shelters that are not tents

If you really want to go simple, discreet and light, then look into bivi-bags.
35 Essentially a waterproof cover for a sleeping bag – with maybe enough room for your rucksack too – they certainly tick the 'small and light' box. Some are exactly as I've just described: when you zip it closed, you'll have a face full of cloth. Some are a bit more structured, with one or two short hoops to lift the fabric clear of you, making something akin to a sleeping-
40 bag-sized tunnel tent. Not everybody's cup of tea, but if you're happy to sacrifice living space of any description, bivis definitely have the advantage over tents. They're light, tiny, frequently made in murky colours, and however severe the wind may be, it's pretty difficult to flatten something that's already flat on the floor!

Source B – 19th century literary non-fiction

From *Travels with a Donkey in the Cévennes* by Robert Louis Stevenson, published in 1879. Here Stevenson explains how he prepared to set out on a long hike on his own.

It was already hard upon October before I was ready to set forth, and at the high altitudes over which my road lay there was no Indian summer to be looked for. A traveller of my sort was a thing hitherto unheard of in that district.

5   I was looked upon with contempt, like a man who should project a journey to the moon. I was determined to have the means of camping out in my possession; for there is nothing more harassing to an easy mind than the necessity of reaching shelter by dusk, and the hospitality

10   of a village inn is not always to be reckoned sure by those who trudge on foot. A tent is troublesome to pitch, and troublesome to strike again. A sleeping-sack, on the other hand, is always ready—you have only to get into it; it serves a double purpose—a bed by night, a portmanteau

15   by day; and it does not advertise your intention of camping out to every curious passer-by. This is a huge point. If a camp is not secret, it is but a troubled resting-place; you become a public character; the convivial rustic visits your bedside after an early supper; and you must sleep with

20   one eye open, and be up before the day. I decided on a sleeping-sack.

This child of my invention was nearly six feet square, exclusive of two triangular flaps to serve as a pillow by night and as the top and bottom of the sack by day. I call it

25   'the sack,' but it was never a sack by more than courtesy: only a sort of long roll or sausage, green waterproof cart-cloth without and blue sheep's fur within. I could bury myself in it up to the neck; for my head I trusted to a fur cap, with a hood to fold down over my ears and a band to

30   pass under my nose like a respirator; and in case of heavy rain I proposed to make myself a little tent, or tentlet, with my waterproof coat, three stones, and a bent branch.

It will readily be conceived that I could not carry this huge package on my own, merely human, shoulders. It

35   remained to choose a beast of burden. What I required was something cheap and small and hardy, and of a stolid and peaceful temper; and all these requisites pointed to a donkey.

Question 1

Here is an example Question 1:

Read again **Source A** from **lines 23 to 32**.

Choose **four** statements below which are TRUE.

- Shade the boxes of the ones that you think are true.
- Choose a maximum of four statements.

[4 marks]

A	Always choose a tent that will be very comfortable to be inside.	
B	The best tent is one that is fairly comfortable to carry and to lie in.	
C	Some people think it is more important for a tent to be comfortable to carry than comfortable to sleep in.	
D	You won't have to carry your tent a long way.	
E	You don't need to worry about how heavy your tent is because most of the time you will be sleeping in it.	
F	Sometimes you will be hiking asleep.	
G	It is important not to draw attention to yourself when you are camping.	
H	A tent that is big and light is a good choice.	

PREPAREIT!

Look at the text extract below, also on the subject of outdoor activities. In the table that follows are some pieces of information we get from the text. Explain how we have to infer information in order to know that the statement is true. One statement is already explained to guide you.

Solo backpacking can be a thrilling experience. However, when planning a trip, throwing caution to the wind is not wise. Attention to detail will keep you safe and happy, and will avoid the misery of humping 25 kilos of unnecessary weight through a mosquito-infested marsh at night.

True statement	Inferred from
Backpacking on your own can be a great experience.	Solo is a synonym for 'on your own'. We need to know that, in order to say the statement is true.
It is wise to plan carefully.	
Your safety and happiness will depend on good planning.	
Poor planning will lead to avoidable miseries.	

WORKIT!

Here is another example Question 1. A student has chosen one statement that is true.

Read again **Source A** from **lines 1 to 22**.

Choose **four** statements below which are TRUE.

- Shade the boxes of the statements that you think are true.
- Choose a maximum of four statements. **[4 marks]**

> Statement A is true. Here are the words from Source A that prove the statement: '... that's not the end of the story'. You have to interpret a colloquial expression to realise that you are being told that there is more to shelter than just tents.

A	There is more to shelter than a tent.	
B	There is no need to worry about the weight of items you take with you.	
C	Sleep is not very important when you are wild camping.	
D	There are different ways of cooking food when you are wild camping.	
E	Your rucksack should only be as big as absolutely necessary.	
F	All wild campers think tents are essential.	
G	Tents should be a colour that makes them noticeable.	
H	Wild camping tents should not be orange.	

DOIT!

Find and shade the box next to the remaining three true statements. Underline the words in **Source A** which provide the best evidence for the statement.

NAILIT!

Read carefully, inferring information where necessary. Only mark the number of boxes you are asked to – the ones next to the true statements.

DOIT!

Read again **Source A** from **lines 23 to 32**.

Choose **four** statements below which are TRUE.

- Shade the boxes of the ones that you think are true.
- Choose a maximum of four statements. **[4 marks]**

A	Always choose a tent that will be very comfortable to be inside.	
B	The best tent is one that is fairly comfortable to carry and to lie in.	
C	Some people think it is more important for a tent to be comfortable to carry than comfortable to sleep in.	
D	You won't have to carry your tent a long way.	
E	You don't need to worry about how heavy your tent is because most of the time you will be sleeping in it.	
F	Sometimes you will be hiking asleep.	
G	It is important not to draw attention to yourself when you are camping.	
H	A tent that is big and light is a good choice.	

Question 2

Here is an example Question 2:

> You need to refer to **Source A** and **Source B** for this question.
>
> Use details from **both** Sources. Write a summary of the similarities between the preparations for sleeping outdoors advised in Source A and described in Source B.
>
> **[8 marks]**

PREPAREIT!

What **two** things are you asked to write about? Tick two boxes.

Similarities ☐

Differences ☐

Similarities and differences ☐

Preparations for sleeping outdoors ☐

The best time to go camping ☐

NAILIT!

In the exam you will be asked about similarities **or** differences **or** a combination of the two.

Find and underline details in both Source A and Source B that relate to these two things.

PLANIT!

Use the table below to identify **similar** information from the two sources. The table is partly filled in for you.

Aspect of preparation	Source A	Source B	What's similar? What can I infer?
Shelter	Some are opposed to tents.		
Carrying equipment			
Being discreet	'blend in'; 'not be noticed'; 'unobtrusive'	'secret' camp; not carrying a tent 'does not advertise your intention of camping'	Neither of them wants the camp to be noticed by others.
Sleeping without a tent			

DOIT!

Now have a go at answering the question in full. Use the space provided below and then continue on your own writing paper.

....

....

....

....

....

....

....

....

....

....

....

....

....

....

....

....

....

....

....

....

....

....

NAILIT!

In this exam a 'summary' means a simple and accurate explanation in your own words (but perhaps with some very brief quotations). Use appropriate connecting words and phrases to point out similarities or differences: for example, however, whereas, just as, like, in the same way, and so on.

DO IT!

Here is another example question for you to answer. It uses the two sources you have been working on.

Write your answer in the space below and continue on your own paper.

You need to refer to **Source A** and **Source B** for this question.

There are both similarities and differences in the sources' attitudes towards wild camping. Use details from **both** sources to write a summary of the similarities and differences.

[8 marks]

....

....

....

....

....

....

....

....

....

....

....

....

....

....

....

....

....

....

NAILIT!

- Underline the key words in the question. Then in the two sources of information, underline information relating to the key words.
- Use a simple table to bring relevant information together.
- Write about both sources together, or write about one, then the other.

Question 3

KNOWIT!

☞ This question will always be about how the writer of one source uses language to influence the reader. You will need to use relevant subject terminology and details from the text to support your views.

☞ You should spend 12 minutes on this question.

☞ It is worth 12 marks.

Here is an example question:

> You now need to refer **only** to **Source B**, from **line 16** ('This is a huge...') **to the end**.
>
> How does Stevenson use language to convince us that he has prepared well?
>
> **[12 marks]**

PREPAREIT!

You need to be clear about the difference between content and language: in other words, the difference between *what* is said and *how* it is said. Here are six statements that might be used in an answer to the question above. However, two of the statements are only about *content*, not *language*. Shade those two statements:

A	He gives a lot of reasons why you must not let people know you will be camping.	
B	He uses a sudden short sentence in order to sound decisive and as though he knows what he is talking about.	
C	He uses metaphors to make his descriptions more appealing.	
D	He uses lists of details that build in momentum, making it sound like he has everything covered.	
E	He mentions lots of ways to sleep warmly and comfortably.	
F	He uses a semicolon to separate a problem and his solution, thus creating suspense before the solution, so that it surprises us and makes it sound clever and original.	

NAILIT!

Writing about language means mentioning some specific techniques and commenting on their **effect**.

NAILIT!

Write only about the part of the source that is given in the question.

PLANIT!

Use the table below to analyse some language techniques you find in Source B. Some of the table has been filled in to help you.

Language feature	Example	Effect
Sudden short sentence	'I decided on a sleeping-sack.'	Coming at the end of a long sentence full of problems, the shortness of this sentence sounds decisive and as though he knows what he is talking about.
Metaphor		

DOIT!

Now have a go at writing the answer to the question. Continue on your own paper.

....
....
....
....
....
....
....
....
....
....

DO IT!

Here is another example Question 3 for you to answer. Use the space below and continue on your own paper.

You now need to refer **only** to **Source B,** from the **beginning to line 21**.

How does Stevenson use language to show his feelings about the trip he is planning?

[12 marks]

Question 4

KNOWIT!

☞ Question 4 will ask you to consider how the writers in both sources **convey** their **ideas** and **perspectives**. You must choose evidence from the text to support your response.

☞ You should spend 16 minutes on this question.

☞ It is worth 16 marks.

Here is an example Question 4:

For this question, you need to refer to the **whole of Source A,** together with **Source B**.

Compare how the two writers convey their different views and experiences of camping and hiking.

In your answer, you could:

• compare their different views and experiences

• compare the methods they use to convey those views and experiences

• support your ideas with references to both texts.

[16 marks]

PREPAREIT!

Annotate the question above so that you understand what you are being asked to do. Think about:

• What is the focus of the question?

• What parts of the sources should you use?

• What must you do?

NAILIT!

Make sure you leave yourself 16 minutes to plan and write a full and thoughtful answer. Spend 4 minutes preparing the question and planning your answer.

NAILIT!

Convey means send or communicate. The question will always be about **how** the writers express their point of view. **How** is about **method**.

PLANIT!

After you have prepared the question for one minute, you should plan your answer. Here is a plan started by another student. Add further evidence supporting **different** views and experiences.

	Source A	Source B
Views	Confident, friendly and humorous	Sounds a bit resentful
Experiences	Sounds very experienced	Has had experience it seems
Details/evidence	Often informal ('a good bet')	Uses present tense to shift into advice rather than narrative: 'A tent is...' Shows wisdom of experience

NAILIT!

Plan your answer either by using a comparison and evidence chart, or – more informally – by annotating the source itself, underlining details and writing notes in the margin.

DO IT!

Write your answer to the question about how the two writers convey their different views and experiences of camping and hiking. Continue on your own paper.

DO IT!

Here is another question for you to answer. Use the space below and continue on your own paper.

For this question, you need to refer to the **whole of Source A**, together with **Source B**.

Compare how the two writers convey their different attitudes to wild camping.

In your answer, you could:

- compare their attitudes
- compare the methods they use to convey those attitudes
- support your ideas with references to both texts.

[16 marks]

....
....
....
....
....
....
....
....
....
....
....
....
....
....
....
....
....
....
....
....
....

Paper 2 Section B: Writing
Introduction and advice

☞ The exam question will ask you to express your own **personal viewpoint** on a topic that is linked to the texts in the reading section of Paper 2.

☞ There will be just one writing task: you will **not** have a choice.

☞ You should spend 45 minutes on the planning and writing.

☞ There are 40 marks for the writing task.

   • 24 of the marks are for content and organisation.

   • 16 of the marks are for technical accuracy – spelling, vocabulary, punctuation and grammar (see page 61).

☞ The question (the task) will give you a specific audience (reader). For example, you might be asked to write to parents, a school governor or the readers of a local newspaper.

☞ The question will also state a purpose and a form from the following lists:

Purposes	Forms
• to explain (a point of view)	• a letter
• to instruct or advise	• an article (such as, for a newspaper)
• to argue	
• to persuade	• the text for a leaflet
	• a speech

Here are some examples of a Question 5:

'The internet can be a very unsafe place for children. Parents should supervise their children's use of computers and smart phones.'

Write the text for a leaflet advising parents on how they can help to protect their children's safety online.

(24 marks for content and organisation
16 marks for technical accuracy)
[40 marks]

'The government must control the amount of fat and sugar young people eat and drink. Obesity is too big an issue to be left to individuals to make their own decisions.'

Write a speech for a debating competition judged by teachers, arguing for or against this statement.

(24 marks for content and organisation
16 marks for technical accuracy)
[40 marks]

NAILIT!

Aim to spend your time as follows:

- 5 minutes preparing and planning
- 35 minutes writing
- 5 minutes checking and correcting.

NAILIT!

Make sure you:

- identify the audience, purpose and form
- make sense of the statement
- are clear about exactly what you must do.

WORKIT!

Here is an example of how a student has 'marked up' a question to prepare it.

> **Statement to stir up my opinion: youth, rights, futures (emotive words)**
>
> 'The age for voting in elections should be lowered to 16. Young people should have the right to vote on the issues that will influence their future lives.'
>
> **Purpose**
>
> Write an article for your local newspaper in which you explain your point of view on this statement.
>
> **Form**
>
> **Audience**
>
> **I need to explain my views on whether the voting age should go down to 16. Keep it formal.**

The student has read the statement carefully and has identified the audience, purpose and form in the question. The student has made a clear note about what they have to do, to avoid misreading the question.

PREPAREIT!

Choose one of the examples of a Question 5 and think about the following carefully.

Who is the audience? _____

What is the subject matter? _____

What form is needed? _____

What is the purpose? _____

DOIT!

Now annotate the Question 5 that you have chosen with some ideas.

PLANIT!

Below is a student's quick six-paragraph plan in answer to the question about lowering the voting age. Note that the plan includes ideas as well as notes on suitable language and tone.

Introduction: Say I'm in favour. Show that I've thought it through and have a number of reasons. Sound reasonable/thoughtful. Each reason will be a paragraph (below). After a great deal of thought/although I realise that... Mention a recent national vote.
Point 1: Responsibility and pressures - GCSE, education. We must be mature enough.
Point 2: How can we take responsibility if we are not allowed to take part in the decisions that will determine our futures? (but be respectful to older people and their judgement)
Point 3: They had vote at 16 in the Scottish referendum. Need to be consistent. Wasn't a disaster.
Point 4: It's our future. Result of vote will have even more impact on our young lives. (Acknowledge other side to show I've thought it through: 'While some people will say that...' However... Despite that... If it's really true that... then.) Don't be too pushy.
Conclusion: The most important point... Maturity? Responsibility? Strong 'sign off'. Refer back to first paragraph for neatness.

Now create your a plan for your chosen question in the space provided below.

WORKIT!

Read these three different opening paragraphs to the question on lowering the voting age to 16:

A

> People who read this newspaper are very interested in politics and they were probably also very interested when they were young so they would probably have wanted to be allowed to vote when they were as young as 16. Nowadays, we have to wait until we are 18 to vote, but why? I am going to explain why I believe that the voting age should be reduced to 16 so that people can get involved in politics from an early age. We need more people to be involved because there are less and less people voting in elections - it's like it's going out of fashion. Getting the voting age down to 16 will create a new zest for the political process and an energised electorate.

B

> I would like to see the voting age lowered to 16. 18-year-olds can vote at the moment but there isn't much difference between an 18-year-old and a 16-year-old. They are really almost the same age. Some 16-year-olds are much more mature than some 18-year-olds even so why can't 16-year-olds have the vote? Give us the vote!

C

> In the recent Scottish referendum on independence, the voting franchise was extended to 16-year-olds. At the time, many older people complained that this would create havoc because young people could not be expected to understand the complex issues involved, and to cast their vote sensibly. However, I would like to argue that far from provoking chaos, extending the vote to younger people has been a great success: it generated excitement around a very important referendum, and it enthused young people about the political process in a way that can only be good for our democracy.

Look at the mark scheme on page 10 and then rank the three paragraphs in order of effectiveness.

NAILIT!

The first paragraph of your writing is crucial. In that opening you need to reassure the exam marker that you can get the right style, tone and vocabulary for the task you have been given.

In the opening you must think carefully about:

- audience
- purpose
- form.

WORKIT!

Here is one paragraph from a student's answer to the question on lowering the voting age. Read the paragraph and the exam marker's notes and comments.

Rather vague vocab – 'old days', 'got'

I/you – engaging, but perhaps too informal

'lower' is clumsy used like this

In the old days almost no one had the vote. More and more people were given the vote during Victorian times and just after. At first men got the vote, and then women above thirty got the vote, and then everyone over twenty-one got the vote. Eventually – I think in the 1970s – the voting age for everyone was lowered to 18. You can see how more and more people and younger and younger people have been given the vote. I think it's inevitable that the voting age will lower to sixteen. If sixteen is not right now, then why was eighteen right many years ago?

This is clearly expressed and the paragraph is effectively organised so that it leads logically to its conclusion. Perhaps the central point – inevitability – should have been at the start though? The language and tone is mainly suitable, although it could be more formal and precise. It could have more authority. Repetition and the final rhetorical question give some force to the argument, but the paragraph is better on persuasion than explanation. This paragraph suggests the answer will just reach into Band 3.

How could you improve this student's answer? Use the space below to rewrite the paragraph so that it is firmly in Band 4.

....
....
....
....
....
....
....
....
....
....
....
....

Technical accuracy

KNOW IT!

☞ The mark scheme for content and organisation covers 24 of the 40 marks for the Paper 2 Section B: writing question.

☞ The other 16 marks are for technical accuracy: **spelling**, **punctuation**, **vocabulary** and **grammar**. You can find the mark scheme for technical accuracy on page 13.

WORK IT!

Below is one paragraph from a student's answer to the question on lowering the voting age. Read the paragraph and the exam marker's comment at the end.

Keep referring back to the mark scheme on page 13.

> The most important thing to consider is not how old a voater is, but how machure they are, some people are old and immachure and some people are young and very machure, instead of giving anyone a voat when they reach a curtain age it might be better to give them a test to find out how sensable they are. Some voaters mite find they fale this test in later life; they woud have to hand back there voat as well as there driving license so there mite be some voaters who are 16 and other ex-voaters who are 75.

The exam marker says:

> The student sometimes uses a comma when they should be ending a sentence with a full stop. However, sentences are well constructed and are often effective: they make the point with force and originality. The semi-colon usefully introduces a connected thought. There is some range of punctuation. The vocabulary hints at some sophistication (voter, sensible, immature) but these more ambitious words are almost always misspelt. For technical accuracy this answer is in Band 2.

In this piece of writing:

- there are 18 spelling mistakes (including some words spelled incorrectly more than once)
- two commas have been used instead of a full stop and a colon
- at least one comma has been missed out.

Use the space below and your own paper if necessary to rewrite the student's paragraph so that it is firmly in Band 4. Look again at the band descriptors, the exam marker's comment and the list of mistakes, and use them to guide your writing. Don't just correct the writing: improve it.

....

....

....

....

....

....

DO IT!

Now write your own opening paragraph below for the question that you prepared and planned on pages 57 and 58.

....

....

....

....

....

....

....

....

....

....

....

....

....

....

....

....

....

....

....

....

....

....

....

NAILIT!

Before you write your paragraph, ask yourself the following questions:

- Have I prepared and planned the question?
- Am I ready to use formal language?
- How will I engage my reader in an appropriate way?
- Am I aware of the mark schemes and how these might help me?

WORKIT!

When you plan your writing, decide the topic of each paragraph, and the best order for these paragraphs.

Here are the second and third paragraphs of a student's writing about lowering the voting age. Next to the writing are some comments by an exam marker:

It would be very arrogant for a young person like me to lecture readers on this subject. After all, I have only been alive for 16 years, so what do I know about the sort of responsibility that probably comes with having children, finding jobs and paying a mortgage? However, what teenagers lack in experience they more than make up for in enthusiasm and determination. When we study for our GCSEs we learn to handle pressure and we learn to make mature decisions that will potentially influence the rest of our lives.

This maturity does not arrive all at once: it comes bit-by-painful bit as we get ourselves ready for the real world of qualifications and careers and we prove ourselves to be worthy of responsibility. But we can only prove ourselves if we are given opportunities. One valuable opportunity is taking a full part in decisions that determine our future, a future which – if we are as lucky as many of you – will stretch into decades ahead. Taking part in elections is a perfect way to become fully responsible citizens. I am convinced – and I hope you will agree – that being trusted with something as important as the vote, will make us more trustworthy people.

Acknowledges opposite view.

Long, well-controlled, flowing sentence for impressive effect.

Contrasting shorter sentence for effect.

Learn… learn: student often uses repetition for effect and to connect ideas.

'This maturity' makes neat link with previous paragraph, and shows development of argument.

Gives central example of an opportunity.

Logical sequencing/ conclusion of ideas makes it hard for the reader to disagree.

This writing targets purpose, form and audience very successfully, as well as meeting requirements for technical accuracy. It is an answer at the top of Band 4.

Now on a separate piece of paper, write your own second and third paragraphs for the question you have been preparing.

DO IT!

Below is another example exam question for you to work on. Use the space below and continue on your own paper.

'The internet has greatly improved our lives. It's hard to imagine how we ever lived without it.'

Write a magazine article in which you explain your point of view on this statement.

(24 marks for content and organisation
16 marks for technical accuracy)

[40 marks]

....

....

....

....

....

....

....

....

....

....

....

....

....

....

....

....

....

....

....

NAILIT!

Make sure you:

- prepare the question
- plan your answer
- write your answer with a good opening and linked paragraphs
- check for technical accuracy.

ENGLISH LITERATURE

Here is a simplified mark scheme for the papers:

Descriptors	Band 3	Band 4	Band 5	Band 6
	The student answer…	The student answer…	The student answer…	The student answer…
AO1 Read, understand and respond Use evidence	• often explains the text in relation to the task • uses references to support a range of relevant comments.	• clearly explains the text in relation to the task • uses references to support explanations effectively.	• thoughtfully explains the text in relation to the task • integrates apt references into the answer.	• critically explains the text in relation to the task • integrates references into the answer very precisely.
AO2 Language, form and structure Subject terminology	• comments on the writer's methods, and the effects these have on the reader • uses some relevant terminology.	• clearly explains the writer's methods, and the effects these have on the reader • uses relevant terminology appropriately.	• effectively explains the writer's methods, and the effects these have on the reader • uses relevant terminology effectively.	• precisely explains the writer's methods, and the effects these have on the reader • uses relevant terminology precisely.
AO3 Contexts (**not** relevant to the unseen poetry question)	• shows some understanding of the significance of context.	• shows a clear understanding of the significance of specific contexts.	• shows a thoughtful consideration of the significance of specific contexts.	• shows a critical consideration of the significance of specific contexts.

Contexts

AO3 (Contexts) is worth far fewer marks than AO1 or AO2, but it is important. You will find some advice on writing about contexts on the following pages.

Spelling, punctuation and grammar (SPaG)

Two questions have four additional marks available for spelling, punctuation and grammar (AO4). To get these marks you must take care to express yourself clearly and accurately.

The two questions tested for SPaG are the Shakespeare question on Paper 1, and the modern texts question on Paper 2.

Paper 1 Section A: Shakespeare

Questions will follow the format below. This question is about *Macbeth:*

Read the following extract from Act 5 Scene 5 of *Macbeth* and then answer the question that follows.

At this point in the play Macbeth is reacting to his wife's death.

MACBETH
I have almost forgot the taste of fears;
The time has been, my senses would have cool'd
To hear a night-shriek; and my fell of hair
5   Would at a dismal treatise rouse and stir
As life were in't: I have supp'd full with horrors;
Direness, familiar to my slaughterous thoughts
Cannot once start me.

Re-enter SEYTON

10 Wherefore was that cry?

SEYTON
The queen, my lord, is dead.

MACBETH
She should have died hereafter;
15 There would have been a time for such a word.
To-morrow, and to-morrow, and to-morrow,
Creeps in this petty pace from day to day
To the last syllable of recorded time,
And all our yesterdays have lighted fools
20 The way to dusty death. Out, out, brief candle!
Life's but a walking shadow, a poor player
That struts and frets his hour upon the stage
And then is heard no more: it is a tale
Told by an idiot, full of sound and fury,
25 Signifying nothing.

Starting with this moment in the play, do you think Shakespeare presents Macbeth as a thoughtful character?

Write about:

• what Macbeth's thoughts are at this point

• how Shakespeare presents Macbeth's thoughts in the play as a whole.

[30 marks]

AO4 [4 marks]

All of the questions in this section will follow this format and you should use the bullet points to guide you when you write your answer.

Below are some example questions and extract references for all of the Shakespeare plays covered in this section.

Macbeth Act 3 Scene 1 Lines 1–10	Starting with this extract, how does Shakespeare present suspicions about Macbeth? Write about: • how Shakespeare presents Banquo's suspicions in this speech • how Shakespeare presents suspicions about Macbeth in the play as a whole.
Romeo and Juliet Act 1 Scene 5 Line 92 ('If I profane...') to Line 109 ('... my sin again')	Starting with this extract, explain how Shakespeare presents the relationship between Romeo and Juliet. Write about: • how Shakespeare presents the relationship between Romeo and Juliet in this conversation • how Shakespeare presents their relationship in the play as a whole.
Much Ado About Nothing Act 2 Scene 1 Line 50 ('Well niece...') to Line 65 ('... in my kindred')	Starting with this extract, explain how far you think Shakespeare presents Beatrice as a confident and witty woman. Write about: • how Shakespeare presents Beatrice in this conversation • how Shakespeare presents Beatrice in the play as a whole.
The Merchant of Venice Act 1 Scene 2 Line 53 ('God made...') to Line 72 ('... behaviour everywhere')	Starting with this extract, explain how far you think Shakespeare presents Portia as an independent woman. Write about: • how Shakespeare presents Portia in this conversation • how Shakespeare presents Portia in the play as a whole.
The Tempest Act 4 Scene 1 Line 147 (Be cheerful...) to Line 169 (... brain is troubled)	Starting with this extract, explore how Shakespeare presents the limits of Prospero's power. Write about: • how Shakespeare presents Prospero's powers in this speech • how Shakespeare presents Prospero's powers in the play as a whole.
Julius Caesar Act 1 Scene 3 Line 19 ('Besides...') to Line 32 ('... they point upon')	Starting with this extract, write about how Shakespeare explores fate in *Julius Caesar*. Write about: • how Shakespeare presents attitudes towards fate in this speech • how Shakespeare presents the role of fate in the play as a whole.

NAILIT!

• Read the question **before** you read the extract to give you a clear focus for your reading.

• Go back to the extract and spend at least five minutes reading it carefully and making some notes that are likely to be relevant to the question.

• Don't ignore the bullet points in the question. They are there to help you be relevant.

WORKIT!

It is important that you really understand the question and what it is asking you to do. You should 'prepare' the question.

Here is how one student prepared the question on *Macbeth*. Notice how they have underlined key words and made some notes about their first thoughts. This will help them to keep their answer sharp and relevant.

> To what extent do I think he is thoughtful?

> Key words underlined.
> He often thinks at length – soliloquies. He often hesitates/overthinks.

Starting with this moment in the play, do you think Shakespeare presents <u>Macbeth</u> as a <u>thoughtful</u> character?

Write about:

> Choose three key bits: hears he is Thane of Cawdor; hesitates over killing Duncan; impulsive/rash towards the end.

- what Macbeth's thoughts are at this point

> Analyses himself/ philosophical

- how Shakespeare presents Macbeth's thoughts in the play as a whole.

MACBETH
I have almost forgot the taste of fears;
The time has been, my senses would have cool'd
To hear a night-shriek; and my fell of hair
5   Would at a dismal treatise rouse and stir
As life were in't: I have supp'd full with horrors;
Direness, familiar to my slaughterous thoughts
Cannot once start me.

> Thinking here... Very self-analytical... cool, detached thinking.
>
> Many of his harsh words and images contrast with the coolness of his thoughts.

Re-enter SEYTON

10   Wherefore was that cry?

SEYTON
The queen, my lord, is dead.

MACBETH
She should have died hereafter;
15   There would have been a time for such a word.
To-morrow, and to-morrow, and to-morrow,
Creeps in this petty pace from day to day
To the last syllable of recorded time,
And all our yesterdays have lighted fools
20   The way to dusty death. Out, out, brief candle!
Life's but a walking shadow, a poor player

> Bitter mood

That struts and frets his hour upon the stage
And then is heard no more: it is a tale
Told by an idiot, full of sound and fury,
25   Signifying nothing.

PREPAREIT!

Select a question from page 67 and make some notes to prepare it, as shown in the example on page 68. You can either base your answer on the extract suggested, or select a different passage from the play, which you can use to give evidence in support of your ideas.

Use the space below to prepare your question.

PREPAREIT!

PLANIT!

Once you have prepared the question, you should spend a few minutes planning the outline of your answer. This plan should be about:

- key ideas to include
- the content of each paragraph
- the order of the paragraphs.

Don't forget to:

- take note of the bullet points in the question
- compare the extract with two or three other relevant points in the text
- use evidence and subject terminology.

Below on the left is one student's plan for their answer to the question about Macbeth as a thoughtful character.

Paragraph 1
Write about the extract: Macbeth's thinking/state of mind here.
Paragraph 2
Vivid words/images; repetition; extended metaphor of 'player'.
Paragraph 3
Early in play when he reacts to news about promotion: "Look how our partner's rapt" (Banquo).
Paragraph 4
Decides not to kill Duncan: 'If it were done...' speech. His conscience.
Paragraph 5
Decision to slaughter Macduff and family 'before this purpose cool'.

Now use the boxes below to plan an answer to the question you have been preparing for *your* Shakespeare text.

Paragraph 1
Paragraph 2
Paragraph 3
Paragraph 4
Paragraph 5

WORKIT!

Here is part of one student's answer to the question about Macbeth as a thoughtful character. In the margin you will find a few notes made by an exam marker.

> **Very obvious, but good point!**

> **But what sort of thinker?**

...Shakespeare gives Macbeth soliloquies when he is speaking to himself, so he must be very thoughtful because no one is listening. In this speech, he uses many words to show the strength of his thoughts about how much he has changed: he knows he has 'supped full of horrors'. Putting supping (eating) and horrors together is shocking for the audience, and 'direness' and 'slaughterous' are equally vivid and emotive words that add to the shock for the audience, who have to know that this man is a deep thinker. It's like his mind is possessed. Of course audiences then might have been even more impressed then than they are now because a belief in the supernatural was probably even stronger. They might have concluded that he was literally possessed by the devil.

We shouldn't be surprised by Macbeth's thoughtfulness because even at the start of the play - when he is surprised by news of his promotion - we discover that he is not just a man of violent action, but also the sort of person who can be paralysed by his thinking. Banquo comments on, 'look how our partner's rapt.' He means that Macbeth has gone into a sort of trance of thinking...

> **Effective choices of quotation, well integrated, but could investigate how at least one of them works on the audience: what are the word's connotations?**

> **Quick consideration of significance of context - audiences in different eras.**

> **Good precise summary of Macbeth's state of mind at this point.**

Look at the checklist on page 72 and the mark scheme on page 65.

- Add to the comments the marker has already made.

- Write some advice in the space below for this student about what they have done well and how they might make their answer even better. Continue on your own paper.

DO IT!

Now using all the tools you have learned, write your own answer to the question you have prepared and planned on the play you have been studying. Try to spend only 40 minutes on your writing. Aim to write at least 500 words. You will need to use your own paper for this.

NAILIT!

Here is a checklist to make your answer as good as possible:

- Prepare and plan.
- Be aware of the mark scheme for literature (see page 65).
- Make clear, relevant points.
- Back up your points with examples, short quotations and other references to the text.
- Make sure you concentrate on *how* Shakespeare puts over his ideas.
- Make a *useful*, relevant point about context.
- Don't forget the marks for spelling, punctuation and grammar.
- When you finish your writing, spend between three and five minutes checking it over. Check that your answer makes sense and that you have not made any careless mistakes with spelling, punctuation and grammar.
- Check that you have used appropriate vocabulary, including subject terminology.

DO IT!

Try constructing your own questions for the play you have studied, based on the list of themes below. Then prepare, plan and answer your questions.

Play	Possible themes
Romeo and Juliet	Love, marriage, conflict, youth and age, reconciliation
The Tempest	Revenge, forgiveness, love, power, fatherhood, justice
The Merchant of Venice	Justice, mercy, race, fatherhood, deception
Julius Caesar	Power, loyalty, plotting, ambition
Macbeth	Evil, power, kingship, heroism, guilt, bravery, the supernatural
Much Ado About Nothing	Jealousy, men and women, love, law and order, loyalty

Paper 1 Section B: The 19th-century novel

KNOWIT!

☞ You will answer one essay question from a choice of two on the 19th-century novel you have studied.

☞ You will be given an extract from your novel, and you will be asked to write about the extract and the whole novel.

☞ Spend 50 minutes on this section of the exam.

☞ There are 30 marks available for this question. There are no marks available for spelling, punctuation and grammar.

Here is an example of the sort of extract and question you might be given. It is from *A Christmas Carol* by Charles Dickens.

Read the following extract from Stave 3 and then answer the question that follows.

In this extract, the second ghost has taken Scrooge to see the shops on Christmas morning.

The people who were shovelling away on the house-tops were jovial and full of glee; calling out to one another from the parapets, and now and then exchanging a facetious snow-ball—better-natured missile far than many a wordy jest—laughing heartily if it went right, and not less
5 heartily if it went wrong. The poulterers' shops were still half open, and the fruiterers were radiant in their glory. There were great, round, pot-bellied baskets of chestnuts, shaped like the waistcoats of jolly old gentlemen, lolling at the doors, and tumbling out into the street in their apoplectic opulence. There were ruddy, brown-faced, broad-girthed
10 Spanish onions, shining in the fatness of their growth like Spanish friars, and winking from their shelves in wanton slyness at the girls as they went by, and glanced demurely at the hung-up mistletoe. There were pears and apples clustered high in blooming pyramids; there were bunches of grapes, made, in the shop-keepers' benevolence, to dangle
15 from conspicuous hooks, that people's mouths might water gratis as they passed; there were piles of filberts, mossy and brown, recalling, in their fragrance, ancient walks among the woods, and pleasant shufflings ankle-deep through withered leaves; there were Norfolk Biffins, squab and swarthy, setting off the yellow of the oranges and
20 lemons, and, in the great compactness of their juicy persons, urgently entreating and beseeching to be carried home in paper bags and eaten after dinner. The very gold and silver fish, set forth among these choice fruits in a bowl, though members of a dull and stagnant-blooded race, appeared to know that there was something going on; and, to a fish, went gasping
25 round and round their little world in slow and passionless excitement.

Starting with this extract, write about how Dickens presents excitement about Christmas.

Write about:

• how Dickens presents Christmas in this extract

• how Dickens presents excitement about Christmas in the novel as a whole.

[30 marks]

All of the questions in this section will follow this format and you should use the bullet points to guide you when you write your answer.

Below are some example questions for all of the 19th-century novels in this section.

Novel	Example question
The Strange Case of Dr Jekyll and Mr Hyde by Robert Louis Stevenson	Read the ending of the novel from 'About a week has passed' to the end. How does Stevenson present Dr Jekyll as a man in torment? Write about: • how Stevenson presents Dr Jekyll in this extract • how Stevenson presents Dr Jekyll's torment and internal conflict in the novel as a whole.
Jane Eyre by Charlotte Brontë	Read Chapter 2 from 'All John Reed's violent tyrannies' to 'general opprobrium.' To what extent does Brontë present Jane as a victim? Write about: • how Brontë presents Jane in this extract • how Brontë presents Jane as a victim in the novel as a whole.
Pride and Prejudice by Jane Austin	Read Chapter 56 from 'Not so hasty' to 'contempt of the world'. How does Austen present attitudes towards social status in *Pride and Prejudice*. Write about: • how Austen presents attitudes towards social status in this extract • how Austen presents attitudes towards social status in the novel as a whole.
A Christmas Carol by Charles Dickens	Read from Stave 2: The First of the Three Spirits when Scrooge's sister comes to bring him home from 'It opened; and a little girl' to 'accompanied her.' Explain how Dickens explores the importance of family in *A Christmas Carol*. Write about: • how Dickens explores the importance of family in this extract • how Dickens explores the importance of family in the novel as a whole.
Great Expectations by Charles Dickens	Read Chapter 27 when Pip is waiting for Joe's arrival from 'Not with pleasure' to 'quite so brisk about it'. How does Dickens present the importance of appearances and respectability in *Great Expectations*? Write about: • how Dickens present the importance of appearances and respectability in this extract • how Dickens present the importance of appearances and respectability in the novel as a whole
Frankenstein by Mary Shelley	Read The Third Victim from 'Or were they rude to every stranger?' to 'took place last night'. How does Shelley present the effects of prejudice in *Frankenstein*? Write about: • how Shelley present the effects of prejudice in this extract • how Shelley present the effects of prejudice in the novel as a whole.
The Sign of Four by Sir Arthur Conan Doyle	Read Chapter 10 from 'We were fairly after her now' to 'rounding the Isle of Dogs'. Explore how Conan Doyle creates a sense of tension in *The Sign of Four*. Write about: • how Conan Doyle creates a sense of tension in this extract • how Conan Doyle creates a sense of tension in the novel as a whole.

PREPAREIT!

Before you begin answering the question, make sure that you really understand what it is asking you to do. This will help you to keep your answer sharp and relevant.

Here is how one student began preparing the question on *A Christmas Carol*:

> The people who were shovelling away on the house-tops were jovial and full of glee; calling out to one another from the parapets, and now and then exchanging a facetious snow-ball—better-natured missile far than many a wordy jest—laughing heartily if it went right, and not less
> 5 heartily if it went wrong. The poulterers' shops were still half open, and the fruiterers were radiant in their glory. There were great, round, pot-bellied baskets of chestnuts, shaped like the waistcoats of jolly old gentlemen, lolling at the doors, and tumbling out into the street in their apoplectic opulence. There were ruddy, brown-faced, broad-girthed
> 10 Spanish onions, shining in the fatness of their growth like Spanish friars, and winking from their shelves in wanton slyness at the girls as they went by, and glanced demurely at the hung-up mistletoe. There were pears and apples clustered high in blooming pyramids; there were bunches of grapes, made, in the shop-keepers' benevolence, to dangle
> 15 from conspicuous hooks, that people's mouths might water gratis as they passed; there were piles of filberts, mossy and brown, recalling, in their fragrance, ancient walks among the woods, and pleasant shufflings ankle-deep through withered leaves ; there were Norfolk Biffins, squab and swarthy, setting off the yellow of the oranges and
> 20 lemons, and, in the great compactness of their juicy persons, urgently entreating and beseeching to be carried home in paper bags and eaten after dinner. The very gold and silver fish, set forth among these choice fruits in a bowl, though members of a dull and stagnant-blooded race, appeared to know that there was something going on; and, to a fish,
> 25 went gasping round and round their little world in slow and passionless excitement.

(margin note, top) All these 'ing' verbs make the fun sound continuous and very active

(margin note, middle) So many images suggest fatness, which suggests plenty and ripeness - 'pot-bellied', 'broad-girthed', 'fatness', and so on.

(margin note, bottom) Excitement, but why does he choose 'passionless'?

Choose the question for the 19th-century novel you are studying from the table on page 74 and 'prepare' the question in the space below.

PLANIT!

Once you have prepared the question on the novel you have studied, spend a few minutes planning the outline of your answer using the boxes below. (You do not have to stick to this number of paragraphs.) This plan should be about:

- key ideas to include
- the content of each paragraph
- the order of the paragraphs.

Paragraph 1

Paragraph 2

Paragraph 3

Paragraph 4

Paragraph 5

Paragraph 6

NAILIT!

Don't forget to:

- take note of the bullet points in the question – they are there to guide you
- compare the extract with two or three other relevant points in the text
- use evidence and subject terminology.

WORKIT!

Here is part of what one student wrote for the question on *A Christmas Carol* with some notes from an exam marker.

One way Dickens makes the Christmas preparations sound exciting is by making a big list of stuff and starting lots of actions with 'ing' words: for example, 'shovelling', 'exchanging', 'laughing'. It makes the action very breathless and full of action. Also there are so many details listed that the reader can hardly keep up. For example, all the different foods are mentioned and described. So there are chestnuts, onions, pears, apples, grapes and other stuff and it's like we are rushing from one to the other and we can't help ourselves.

> Lists – good point.

> Evidence followed by some explanation. Good.

> No mention of how these are described.

Here is what one exam marker wrote about this part of the student's answer.

The answer is quite well organised: it makes good points, provides evidence and points out the effect on the reader. However, the student's own language is too vague and repetitive for the explanations to be very clear. Comments made about effects are useful and sometimes even perceptive (for example, the use of the word 'breathless'), but are too brief: nothing is explored. The answer will probably not get above Band 3.

Use the space below to make more notes about the writing. Pick out words or phrases from the text to back up your points. Refer to the mark scheme on page 65 to guide you.

....
....
....
....
....
....
....
....
....
....
....
....
....
....

DO IT!

Now have a go at answering the question you have been preparing and planning. You should spend 35–40 minutes on your writing and aim to write at least 500 words. Use the space provided below and continue on your own paper.

....

....

....

....

....

....

....

....

....

....

....

....

....

....

....

....

DO IT!

Try constructing your own questions for the novel you have studied, based on this list of themes.

Novel	Some themes
The Strange Case of Dr Jekyll and Mr Hyde	Evil, science, morality, horror, self-awareness
A Christmas Carol	Family, Christmas, greed, social responsibility, kindness, learning
Great Expectations	Love, ambition, self-improvement, social class, guilt, innocence
Jane Eyre	Love, independence, the position of women, marriage, education, justice, class
Frankenstein	Science, horror, mankind, nature, evil, prejudice
Pride and Prejudice	Social class, marriage, women, love, ambition, respectability
The Sign of Four	Evil, fear, empire, justice

Paper 2 Section A: Modern texts

KNOWIT!

☞ You will answer one essay question from a choice of two on your studied modern prose or drama text.

☞ You will have studied one of the following texts:

JB Priestley	An Inspector Calls
Willy Russell	Blood Brothers
Alan Bennett	The History Boys
Dennis Kelly	DNA
Simon Stephens	The Curious Incident of the Dog in the Night-Time
Shelagh Delaney	A Taste of Honey
William Golding	Lord of the Flies
AQA Anthology	Telling Tales
George Orwell	Animal Farm
Kazuo Ishiguro	Never Let Me Go
Meera Syal	Anita and Me
Stephen Kelman	Pigeon English

☞ You should spend 45 minutes on this section.

☞ The question is worth 30 marks.

☞ There are four additional marks for AO4: use a range of vocabulary and sentence structures for clarity, purpose and effect, with accurate spelling and punctuation.

Questions will follow the format below. This question is about *An Inspector Calls*.

In *An Inspector Calls,* Mr Birling says: 'a man… has to look after himself'. How does Priestley use the character of Mr Birling to explore ideas about the individual in society?

Write about:

- how Priestley presents the character of Mr Birling
- how Priestley uses Mr Birling to explore ideas about individuals in society.

[30 marks]

AO4 [4 marks]

All of the questions in this section will follow this format and you should use the bullet points to guide you when you write your answer.

Below are some example questions for all of the modern texts in this section.

JB Priestley *An Inspector Calls*	To what extent is Gerald changed by the events of *An Inspector Calls*? Write about: • how Gerald reacts to the inspector's visit • how Priestley presents Gerald by the way he writes.
Willy Russell *Blood Brothers*	How does Russell present freedom in *Blood Brothers*? Write about: • the ways particular characters struggle for freedom • how Russell presents freedom by the way he writes.
Alan Bennett *The History Boys*	How does Bennett present different ideas about education in *The History Boys?* Write about: • the different attitudes towards education in the play • how Bennett uses these different attitudes to explore ideas about education in *The History Boys.*
Dennis Kelly *DNA*	How does Kelly present the power of speech in *DNA?* Write about: • how characters use talk to have a strong effect on other characters • how Kelly uses these characters to explore ideas about the power of speech.
Simon Stephens *The Curious Incident of the Dog in the Night-Time*	How does the relationship between Christopher and his father change and develop in *The Curious Incident of the Dog in the Night-Time?* Write about: • how Christopher reacts to his father • how Stephens presents the relationship between Christopher and his father by the way he writes.
Shelagh Delaney *A Taste of Honey*	How does Delaney explore responsibility in *A Taste of Honey?* Write about: • ideas about responsibility in *A Taste of Honey* • how Delaney presents these ideas by the way she writes.
William Golding *Lord of the Flies*	How does the relationship between Ralph and Jack change in *Lord of the Flies?* Write about: • how Ralph and Jack react to each other at first • how and why their relationship changes during the rest of the novel.

AQA Anthology *Telling Tales*	In *The Darkness Out There*, the boy realises, 'you could get people wrong'. How do writers present 'getting people wrong' in *The Darkness Out There* and in one other story from *Telling Tales?* Write about: • some of the ideas about misjudging people presented in the two stories • how the writers present these ideas by the way they write.
George Orwell *Animal Farm*	How do the pigs gain and strengthen their control over the other animals in *Animal Farm*? Write about: • the pigs' actions at some key moments in the novel • how Orwell presents the pigs' control methods by the way he writes.
Kazuo Ishiguro *Never Let Me Go*	How does Ishiguro use the relationship between Kathy and Ruth to explore the importance of friendship in *Never Let Me Go*? Write about: • how Ishiguro presents the relationship between Kathy and Ruth • how Ishiguro uses this relationship to explore ideas about friendship.
Meera Syal *Anita and Me*	How does Syal present ideas about tolerance and kindness in *Anita and Me*? Write about: • how Syal presents examples of tolerance and kindness • how Syal presents ideas about tolerance and kindness by the way she writes.
Stephen Kelman *Pigeon English*	How does Kelman present the importance of decisions in *Pigeon English?* Write about: • decisions and choices that Harri makes • how Kelman presents the importance of decisions by the way he writes.

PREPARE IT!

Make sure that you really understand the question and what it is asking you to do. Choose the question for the modern text you are studying from the tables on pages 80–1 and 'prepare' the question in the space below. You should underline the key words and make a few notes to yourself, pointing out the key aspects of the question.

Here is how one student prepared the question on *An Inspector Calls* by JB Priestley.

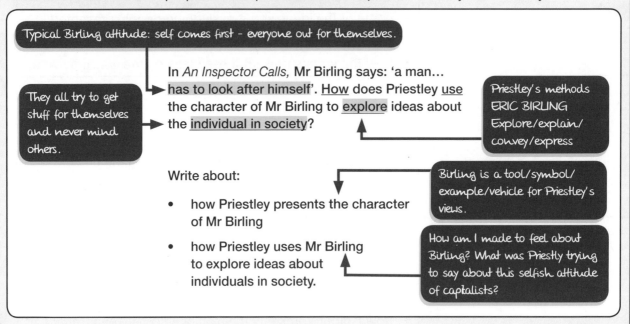

Typical Birling attitude: self comes first – everyone out for themselves.

They all try to get stuff for themselves and never mind others.

In *An Inspector Calls,* Mr Birling says: 'a man… has to look after himself'. How does Priestley use the character of Mr Birling to explore ideas about the individual in society?

Priestley's methods
ERIC BIRLING
Explore/explain/ convey/express

Write about:

- how Priestley presents the character of Mr Birling

- how Priestley uses Mr Birling to explore ideas about individuals in society.

Birling is a tool/symbol/ example/vehicle for Priestley's views.

How am I made to feel about Birling? What was Priestly trying to say about this selfish attitude of capitalists?

Use the space below to prepare your question:

PLANIT!

Once you have prepared your question, you should spend a few minutes planning the outline of your answer.

Below on the left is one student's plan for their answer to the question about how Priestley uses Birling to explore ideas about the individual in society. Use the boxes on the right hand side to plan your own answer to the question that you prepared on page 82.

Intro. Key ideas - Birling is selfish and proud of it. Himself and own family. Others all selfish. He doesn't really change in the play. Contrast with Sheila and Eric.	
How presented - bigot, selfish, destructive. How we feel about how he behaves/what he says. Use of inspector to guide how we react to Birling 'cranks' 'community and all that nonsense' 'a man has to mind his own business'.	
How Birling is used by Priestley. We don't believe/agree with him. He is a bigot. His views are contrasted directly with the inspector. He is made to look stupid, arrogant and dishonest.	
Are there some key methods Priestley uses? Juxtaposition/contrast? Dramatic irony? Birling being set up by Priestley?	
What is the Priestley trying to highlight about people's attitudes towards individuals? Why was this a key concern at that time?	

NAILIT!

- Your plan should be about the content of each paragraph, the order of the paragraphs, evidence to support your points and key ideas to include.
- You need to get quick and efficient at planning.
- Spend only 7–10 minutes on preparing the question and planning the answer.

WORKIT!

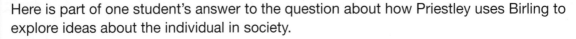

Here is part of one student's answer to the question about how Priestley uses Birling to explore ideas about the individual in society.

> Mr Birling's 'look after himself' speech echoes right through the play, almost drumming it into us, making us dislike Birling more every time he opens his mouth. When the inspector says a completely different speech as he leaves them all – 'we are responsible for each other' – this contradicts what Mr Birling said and makes us side against him even more. Priestley makes us agree that not only must a man 'look after himself and his own' but also treat others as friends, just like you would want others to treat you.
>
> Towards the end of the play, the inspector tells the family that if they haven't learned any lessons tonight then they would be 'taught it in fire and blood and anguish'. Basically, Priestley is saying they will have to learn the hard way, watching family go through the same torture that Eva Smith went through. Also the words 'fire and blood and anguish' relate to the horrors of the First World War that the characters didn't know was about to start. The play was written much later than it is set so the audience knows that the inspector's horrible prediction is right, even though Birling earlier called this prediction 'fiddlesticks'. This dramatic irony helped us to see Birling as blind and stupid.

Look at the mark scheme on page 65. Write some advice for this student about what they have done well and how they might make their answer even better.

....

....

....

....

....

....

....

....

....

....

....

....

....

....

NAILIT!

Here is a checklist for making your answer as developed as possible:
- Prepare and plan your answer.
- Be aware of the mark schemes for English Literature (see page 65 for a simplified mark scheme).
- Make clear, relevant points.
- Support your points with examples, quotations and other references to the text.
- Make sure you concentrate on *how* the writer puts across their ideas.
- Make a thoughtful, relevant point about context for each point.
- When you have finished your writing, spend at least 5 minutes checking that your answer makes sense and that there are no careless mistakes with spelling, punctuation and grammar.
- Check that you have used appropriate vocabulary, including subject terminology.

DO IT!

Now write your own answer to the question you prepared and planned earlier. Spend only 35 minutes on your writing, so that you do not steal time from sections B and C. Aim to write three to four detailed paragraphs, with an introduction and conclusion. Use the space provided below and continue on your own paper.

Paper 2 Section B: Poetry

Here are some example questions:

Love and relationships

Compare how poets present feelings of sadness in 'When We Two Parted' and in **one** other poem from 'Love and relationships'.

[30 marks]

Power and conflict

Compare how poets present attitudes towards violence in 'War Photographer' and in **one** other poem from 'Power and conflict'.

[30 marks]

PREPAREIT!

Make sure that you really understand the question and what it is asking you to do. Choose the question for the cluster you have been studying and 'prepare' the question in the space below. You should underline the key words and make a few notes to yourself, pointing out the key aspects of the question.

Here is how a student prepared a 'Love and relationships' poetry anthology question.

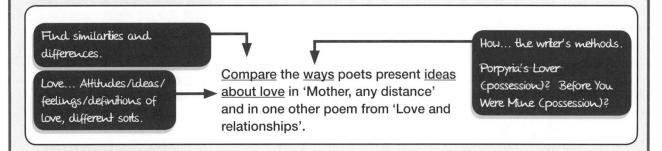

Find similarities and differences.

Love... Attitudes/ideas/ feelings/definitions of love, different sorts.

Compare the ways poets present ideas about love in 'Mother, any distance' and in one other poem from 'Love and relationships'.

How... the writer's methods.

Porpyria's Lover (possession)? Before You Were Mine (possession)?

Use the space below to prepare your question. Don't forget to think about the context.

WORKIT!

The named poem will be printed on the exam paper, so do your quick plan on the exam paper. Write the name of your chosen poem next to the printed poem and then make some notes like in the example below:

Mother, any distance greater than a single span

Mother, any distance greater than a single span
requires a second pair of hands.
You come to help me measure windows, pelmets, doors,
the acres of the walls, the prairies of the floors.

5   You at the <u>zero-end</u>, me with the spool of tape, recording
length, reporting metres, centimetres back to <u>base</u>, then
leaving up the stairs, the line still feeding out,
unreeling years between us. <u>Anchor. Kite</u>.

I space-walk through the empty bedrooms, climb
10   the ladder to the loft, to breaking point, where something
has to give;
two floors below your fingertips still pinch
the last one-hundredth of an inch...I reach
towards a hatch that opens on an endless sky
15   to fall or fly.

Simon Armitage

Before You Were Mine also has single word sentence - Marilyn. These might suggest some contempt? Mockery? Not fully engaged?

Is she left with nothing - zero?

'base' - security? Control?

Single word sentences

Ideas about love

- Is love an anchor (restriction) or a kite (freedom) - fall or fly? Mother's love provides the anchor that makes flight/escape/freedom possible?

- Mother - child love: who has the upper hand?

- Child possesses the mother ('mine'). Photos 'capture' the past/the mother.

PLANIT!

Plan the answer to your question in the space provided below:

Named poem	Chosen poem

NAILIT!

Practise planning. However, don't spend more than 5–6 minutes on this in the exam.

WORKIT!

Here is part of the same student's answer with some comments by an exam marker.

In 'Mother, Any Distance' you can feel the way that the speaker feels about his mother; her 'fingertips still pinch the last one-hundredth of an inch' of the tape. This could suggest that she is desperate to hold on to her son but he knows she is losing him. He keeps contrasting her love and the freedom that he reaches towards: she is the 'anchor' to his 'kite', and in the final **stanza** he reaches upwards towards the 'endless sky'. She is the 'base' and is 'below' while he is reaching out and up. It's as though he almost resents her maternal help and love. And finds it a burden. This **theme** of tension in mother-child love is also in 'Before You Were Mine'.

Integrated evidence.

Evidence explained and explored briefly.

Accurate subject terminology.

Relevant subject terminology.

Look at the mark scheme on page 65. Write some advice for this student about what they have done well and how they might make their answer even better.

....

....

....

....

....

....

....

....

....

....

....

....

....

....

....

....

....

DO IT!

Now write an answer to the question you prepared. Start by writing one paragraph in which you use evidence, subject terminology and make a helpful reference to context. Continue on your own paper.

....
....
....
....
....
....
....
....
....
....
....
....
....
....
....
....
....
....

DO IT!

Here are two more questions for you to work on:

Compare how poets present ideas about togetherness in 'Love's Philosophy' and in **one** other poem from 'Love and relationships'.

[30 marks]

Compare the ways poets present ideas about violence in 'My Last Duchess' and in **one** other poem from 'Power and conflict'.

[30 marks]

Paper 2 Section C: Unseen poetry

KNOWIT!

☞ You will be given poems that you have not seen before. To prepare for the unseen poetry section of the exam you should read a wide range of poetry in order to develop your ability to closely analyse unseen poems.

☞ You will need to be able to analyse and compare key features such as their content, theme, structure and use of language.

☞ There are two questions and you must answer both of them.

☞ You should spend 50 minutes on this section.

☞ Section C is worth 32 marks.

Question 1

☞ You will be given a poem you have not seen before and you will be asked a question about it.

☞ Spend 35 minutes on this question.

☞ It is worth 24 marks.

☞ Try to write three significant paragraphs.

Here is an example of Question 1:

Your Dad Did What? ◀

Where they have been, if they have been away,
or what they've done at home, if they have not –
you make them write about the holiday.
One writes *My Dad did*. What? Your Dad did what?

5   That's not a sentence. Never mind the bell.
We stay behind until the work is done.
You count their words (you who can count and spell);
all the assignments are complete bar one

and though this boy seems bright, that one is his.
10   He says he's finished, doesn't want to add
anything, hands it in just as it is.
No change. *My Dad did*. What? What did his Dad?

You find the 'E' you gave him as you sort
through reams of what this girl did, what that lad did,
15   and read the line again, just one 'e' short:
This holiday was horrible. My Dad did.

                                Sophie Hannah

Annotations:
- Speaker must be teacher
- This list of things sounds weary – teacher done it loads of times?
- 'make them' sounds bossy and unfeeling

In 'Your Dad Did What?' how does the poet present the speaker's feelings about the boy?

[24 marks]

NAILIT!

The exam question will ask you to consider:

- the theme and meaning of the poem
- the poet's methods
- the poem's mood, feelings and attitude
- how the reader is being made to feel about the topic, the speaker or a theme.

Always read the question before you read the poem. Then you know what to look out for.

PREPAREIT!

Use the space to the right of the poem and the lines below (Your Dad Did What?) to make some notes about the poem and annotate the question.

Use the space below to prepare your question. Don't forget to think about the context.

....

....

....

....

....

....

....

....

....

....

....

....

....

....

....

....

....

WORKIT!

Here is part of one student's answer to the question on page 92:

> In the first two stanzas the speaker (the teacher) sounds fed up and frustrated with the boy. I think this is because some of the lines sound like a teacher being naggy: 'that's not a sentence' and 'never mind the bell'. It's just like a teacher going on, but the boy is supposed to be writing about something sensitive and personal. When it then says 'We stay behind until the work is done' it gets worse because now the teacher is being threatening and the 'we' sounds sarcastic. I think the poem makes the speaker's feelings sound bad and makes us against her, so we are on the boy's side.

Now look at what an exam marker says about what this student has written:

> There are strengths in this answer: the student pays attention to detail in the poem and uses evidence (quotations). Also the student notices the feelings of the speaker, and goes on to consider how the reader is likely to feel about the speaker. The answer could be better organised, with one point being made and explained at a time, and some of the student's own language is too everyday to be clear. For example, 'it's just like a teacher going on' is not entirely clear, so that we can't be sure what the student means.

Rewrite the student's answer to improve it. Take into account:

- what the exam marker wrote
- the mark schemes for English Literature (see page 65 for a simplified mark scheme)
- the notes you made on the poem.

Continue on your own paper if necessary.

....
....
....
....
....
....
....
....
....
....
....
....

DO IT!

Here is another example first question on the same poem for you to try. Use the space provided and continue on your own paper.

In 'Your Dad Did What?' how does the poet present the relationship between teachers and students?

[24 marks]

....

....

....

....

....

....

....

....

....

....

....

....

....

....

....

....

....

....

....

....

....

....

....

KNOWIT!
Question 2

☞ You will be given another poem and you will be asked to compare it with the first poem.

☞ It is worth 8 marks.

☞ You should spend 15 minutes on this question.

Here is an example of Question 2:

The Lesson

'Your father's gone,' my bald headmaster said.
His shiny dome and brown tobacco jar
Splintered at once in tears. It wasn't grief.
I cried for knowledge which was bitterer
5   Than any grief. For there and then I knew
That grief has uses – that a father dead
Could bind the bully's fist a week or two;
And then I cried for shame, then for relief.

I was a month past ten when I learnt this:
10 I still remember how the noise was stilled
in school-assembly when my grief came in.
Some goldfish in a bowl quietly sculled
Around their shining prison on its shelf.
They were indifferent. All the other eyes
15 Were turned towards me. Somewhere in myself

Pride, like a goldfish, flashed a sudden fin.

Edward Lucie-Smith

Both 'Your Dad Did What' and 'The Lesson' present students' experiences of school. What are the similarities and/or differences between the ways the poets present those experiences?

[8 marks]

PREPAREIT!
Use the space next to the poem to make some notes that will help you to answer the question.

NAILIT!

Remember: you only have a few minutes for this question, so spend no more than five minutes reading and annotating the poem, and deciding on a couple of **relevant** similarities and/or differences between the two poems.

PLANIT!

Add a few of your own ideas to the chart below:

Your Dad Did What	Both poems	The Lesson

DOIT!

Now write your answer. Aim to write two points of comparison. Continue on your own paper.

....

....

....

....

....

....

....

....

DOIT!

Here is another example question for you to practise. Use your own paper.

Both 'Your Dad Did What' and 'The Lesson' present a student's grief and the teacher's response. What are the similarities and/or differences between the ways the poets present those experiences?

[8 marks]

ENGLISH LANGUAGE
Paper 1 Explorations in creative reading and writing
Time allowed: 1 hour 45 minutes

Source A

This extract is from a novel by George Orwell. It was written and set in the 1930s. Dorothy is the daughter of a vicar. In this section she is carrying out her duty of visiting local people (parishioners) in their homes.

A Clergyman's Daughter

It was a little after eleven. The day, which, like some overripe but hopeful widow playing at seventeen, had been putting on unseasonable April airs, had now remembered that it was August and settled down to be boiling hot.

5 Dorothy rode into the hamlet of Fennelwick, a mile out of Knype Hill. She had delivered Mrs Lewin's corn-plaster, and was dropping in to give old Mrs Pither that cutting from the Daily Mail about angelica tea for rheumatism. The sun, burning in the cloudless sky, scorched her back through her gingham frock, and the dusty road quivered in the heat, and the hot, flat meadows, over which even at this time of year numberless larks chirruped tiresomely, were so green that it hurt your eyes to look at them. It was the kind of day that is called 'glorious'
10 by people who don't have to work.

Dorothy leaned her bicycle against the gate of the Pithers' cottage, and took her handkerchief out of her bag and wiped her hands, which were sweating from the handle-bars. In the harsh sunlight her face looked pinched and colourless. She looked her age, and something over, at that hour of the morning. Throughout her day — and in general it was a seventeen-hour day —
15 she had regular, alternating periods of tiredness and energy; the middle of the morning, when she was doing the first instalment of the day's 'visiting', was one of the tired periods.

'Visiting', because of the distances she had to bicycle from house to house, took up nearly half of Dorothy's day. Every day of her life, except on Sundays, she made from half a dozen to a dozen visits at parishioners' cottages. She penetrated into cramped interiors and sat
20 on lumpy, dust-diffusing chairs gossiping with overworked, blowsy housewives; she spent hurried halfhours giving a hand with the mending and the ironing, and read chapters from the Gospels, and readjusted bandages on 'bad legs', and condoled with sufferers from morning-sickness; she played ride-a-cock-horse with sour-smelling children who grimed the bosom of her dress with their sticky little fingers; she gave advice about ailing aspidistras*,
25 and suggested names for babies, and drank 'nice cups of tea' innumerable — for the working women always wanted her to have a 'nice cup of tea', out of the teapot endlessly stewing.

Much of it was profoundly discouraging work. Few, very few, of the women seemed to have even a conception of the Christian life that she was trying to help them to lead. Some of them were shy and suspicious, stood on the defensive, and made excuses when urged to
30 come to Holy Communion†; some shammed piety for the sake of the tiny sums they could wheedle out of the church alms box; those who welcomed her coming were for the most part

the talkative ones, who wanted an audience for complaints about the 'goings on' of their husbands, or for endless mortuary tales ('And he had to have glass chubes let into his veins,' etc., etc.) about the revolting diseases their relatives had died of. Quite half the women on
35   her list, Dorothy knew, were at heart atheistical in a vague unreasoning way. She came up against it all day long — that vague, blank disbelief so common in illiterate people, against which all argument is powerless. Do what she would, she could never raise the number of regular communicants to more than a dozen or thereabouts. Women would promise to communicate, keep their promise for a month or two, and then fall away. With the younger
40   women it was especially hopeless. They would not even join the local branches of the church leagues that were run for their benefit — Dorothy was honorary secretary of three such leagues, besides being captain of the Girl Guides. The Band of Hope and the Companionship of Marriage languished almost memberless, and the Mothers' Union only kept going because gossip and unlimited strong tea made the weekly sewing-parties acceptable. Yes, it was
45   discouraging work; so discouraging that at times it would have seemed altogether futile if she had not known the sense of futility for what it is — the subtlest weapon of the Devil.

*An aspidistra is a houseplant that was popular at the time.

+ Holy Communion is a church service

Section A: Reading

Answer **all** questions in this section.
You should spend about 45 minutes on this section.

(1) Read again the first part of the Source **lines 1 to 10.**
List **four** things from this part of the text that show that it was summer.

[4 marks]

1 ....

....

2 ....

....

3 ....

....

4 ....

....

(2) Look in detail at this extract from **lines 17 to 26** of the Source:

> 'Visiting', because of the distances she had to bicycle from house to house, took up nearly half of Dorothy's day. Every day of her life, except on Sundays, she made from half a dozen to a dozen visits at parishioners' cottages. She penetrated into cramped interiors and sat on lumpy, dust-diffusing chairs gossiping with overworked, blowsy housewives; she spent hurried halfhours giving a hand with the mending and the ironing, and read chapters from the Gospels, and readjusted bandages on 'bad legs', and condoled with sufferers from morning-sickness; she played ride-a-cock-horse with sour-smelling children who grimed the bosom of her dress with their sticky little fingers; she gave advice about ailing aspidistras*, and suggested names for babies, and drank 'nice cups of tea' innumerable — for the working women always wanted her to have a 'nice cup of tea', out of the teapot endlessly stewing.

How does the writer use language here to describe Dorothy's visits?

You could include the writer's choice of:

- words and phrases
- language features and techniques
- sentence forms.

[8 marks]

....

....

....

....

....

....

....

....

....

....

....

....

....

....

Continue on a separate piece of paper.

(3) You now need to think about the **whole** of the **Source**.

This text is from the beginning of the novel.

How has the writer structured the text to interest you as a reader?

You could write about:

- what the writer focuses your attention on at the beginning
- how and why the writer changes this focus as the source develops
- any other structural features that interest you.

[8 marks]

....

....

....

....

....

....

....

....

....

....

....

....

....

....

....

....

....

....

Continue on a separate piece of paper.

(4) Focus this part of your answer on the final paragraph of the Source from **line 27 to the end**.

A student, having read this section of the text, said: 'This part of the text gives me a very clear understanding of Dorothy and her attitudes.'

To what extent do you agree?

In your response, you could:

- consider your own impressions of Dorothy and her attitudes

- evaluate how the writer has created the character of Dorothy

- support your opinions with references to the text.

[20 marks]

Continue on a separate piece of paper.

Section B: Writing

(5) A hospital is planning a booklet of creative writing under the title 'Just visiting'.

You have been asked to contribute some writing for the booklet, which will be edited by a doctor.

Either:

Write a description suggested by this picture:

Or:

Write a story about a visit to someone either at their home or in hospital.

(24 marks for content and organisation
16 marks for technical accuracy)

[40 marks]

....

....

....

....

....

....

....

....

Continue on a separate piece of paper.

ENGLISH LANGUAGE

Paper 2 Writers' viewpoints and perspectives
Time allowed: 1 hour 45 minutes

Source A: 21st century non-fiction
     An article called *No Way Out* by Richard Durant.

Source B: 19th century non-fiction
     A transcript from a newspaper article called 'Narrative of a survivor' published in 1882.

Source A – 21st century non-fiction

33 Miners, Buried Alive for 69 Days: This Is Their Remarkable Survival Story

After an explosion, some miners in Chile find themselves trapped underground.

Where there had always been the long tunnel to light and air, there was now a wall of stone. It was obvious there was no way through. Despite their desperate situation, the men knew they had to stay calm. The decisions they took now would be crucial if they were to have any chance of surviving.

5   They split into two groups. One group would explore the mine's complex tunnel network. Perhaps they would discover another route to the surface. In addition to the normal tunnels through which the miners reached their work stations, there were also occasional much steeper and narrower supply shafts that were used as supply routes for air, water and electricity. In an emergency these shafts could also be used as emergency exits, and were supposed to be fitted with ladders bolted securely to the rock face. In reality, the San José Mine owners had cut costs
10   by not maintaining these escape routes. Many of them were not even fitted with ladders. Just before the two groups went their separate ways, a foreman, Florencio Ávalos, advised a senior miner in the explorer group to stop his companions from eating and drinking all their supplies. What was obvious to Avalos – and what he wanted to keep secret from the men – was that their chances of survival were slim. If they didn't ration their provisions then their chances were zero.

15   The second group headed back to the central refuge – the underground safety area. When they got there their worst fears were confirmed: supplies of air, water and electricity had all been cut off. The miners settled down to conserve their energy, and waited. For hours. The only light came from the dim lamps on their helmets. When those ran down the darkness would be complete. Hunger, thirst and fear closed in on them.

20   Elsewhere, the explorer group had found a jumbo lifter and had used it to cut a hole in a tunnel roof near to where an escape shaft was marked on the map. One of the men, Sepúlveda, stood on the lifter platform and put his head through the hole. To his delight the light from his helmet lamp revealed a rough iron ladder clamped to a shaft wall. He grabbed a rung and, followed by another miner, Raúl Bustos, he began to climb. Going was hard: the miners choked on the thick
25   dust that filled the air; the walls were damp and slippery; and the metal rungs were rusty and insecure. One rung broke off and fell into Sepúlveda's upturned face, gashing his mouth. Despite these difficulties, the two men kept climbing.

Finally they reached the top of the shaft and climbed onto a broad and lightly-shelving rock shelf. Their hopes rose: this was clearly a ramp to the surface. An escape route. But why was it
30   still pitch dark? They took a few steps upwards and almost immediately came up against a solid, continuous wall of rock. Simultaneously the two men felt the hope drain from them. At that moment they knew they were going to die.

They forced themselves to retrace their steps, climbing back down the shaft. From there they searched for another way out. Perhaps there was another, better used shaft. For a long time all they
35   found was the smooth, black, unyielding rock face. Then suddenly their groping hands found a gap leading to another passage that turned almost straight upwards, and they trained their weakening lamps on the walls of the shaft. This one didn't even have a ladder. This was not the escape route.

Source B – 19th century non-fiction

A narrative of a survivor

In 1882, an explosion in a mine in the North-East of England killed 29 miners. On 17 February 1882 the local newspaper – *The Durham Advertiser* - reported the account of a survivor.

I heard a report* which appeared to come right to me from the direction of the shaft. I said to my marrow†, 'What's that?' To which he replied, 'I think it'll be a shot.' I said, 'That's no shot,' and as I spoke a boy came running up and shouted, 'Be sharp out-bye; there's a something happened. All the 'overcast' is blown out'.

5   We went off as hard as we could towards the shaft, other men and lads joining us. As we ran, the dust was so dense that it was like to smother us. We reached the shaft, however, and there we found the tubs all blown about, and the 'way' torn up, and the timbering and brattice piled up in a heap. The first thing we saw was the dead body of a young man which we recognised as that of William Jefferson. We lifted him up and placed him by the side of
10   the way. We then tried to get round to the other side of the shaft, but on our way we came upon the body of a man whose head had been blown off, a terribly mutilated body. One of our party succeeded in getting round, and saw a young boy's foot peeping out from beneath a tub. We all cowered about the shaft, and wondered if we should get out; it was then evident that no one but those about us could be saved.

15   When we had waited from between half-an-hour and an hour, we saw the lights of lamps coming towards us from the direction of the Cross-cut Flat. There were about nine men in this party, and one of them, just as they came up to us, dropped down. The men got him and brought him safely to the shaft where we were. The other eight men were all very bad from after-damp, and asked for something to drink, but of course we could give them nothing. We
20   stood about the pit for someone to come to us. No one else was found there whilst I was at the shaft bottom. These nine men told us that in the cross-cut flat, from which they came, all the boys were killed. When the explosion took place Jacob Soulsby, the deputy-overman in charge of that district, said, 'Tell them (the boys) to wait at the 'Rest' a bit.' They delivered this message, but the boys did not do so, and they were all killed by the choke-damp†.

25   The cage was broken in the shaft, but at length the slings were let down, and we were drawn to bank by them and the 'kibble'. The engineman underground and I got into the slings together. He told me that when the explosion occurred he was blown away from his engine, but he did not appear to be seriously hurt. There were about thirty men and boys drawn up at the bottom of the shaft – gathered up from the various parts of the workings.
30   None of them appeared to be much the worse, although they had all suffered more or less from choke-damp. The engineman and I came to bank in the sidings, but the kibble was afterwards let down and brought the remainder of the men to bank.

*report – loud sound

†marrow – friend

‡choke damp – carbonic acid gas

Section A: Reading

Answer **all** questions in this section.

You should to spend about 45 minutes on this section.

(1) Read again the first part of **Source A** from **lines 1 to 14**.

Choose **four** statements below which are TRUE.

- Shade the boxes of the ones that you think are true.
- Choose a maximum of four statements.

[4 marks]

A   Only one group of miners looked for an escape route.   ☐

B   They all hoped to find a window behind the curtains.   ☐

C   The mining company also made shoes.   ☐

D   The mining company had saved money by providing fewer ladders.   ☐

E   Florencio Ávalos didn't expect to be rescued immediately.   ☐

F   Florencio Ávalos shouted instructions to the other miners.   ☐

G   Luckily, electricity and air were still flowing into the mine.   ☐

H   Electricity, air and water usually came through supply shafts.   ☐

2 You need to refer to **Source A** and **Source B** for this question.

Use details from **both** Sources. Write a summary of the differences between the experience of the miners in England and the miners in Chile.

[8 marks]

....

....

....

....

....

....

....

....

....

....

....

....

....

....

....

....

....

....

....

....

Continue on separate paper.

(3) You now need to refer **only** to **Source A**, the account of the accident in the mine in Chile.

How does the writer use language to try to make the account lively and interesting?

[12 marks]

....

....

....

....

....

....

....

....

....

....

....

....

....

....

....

....

....

....

....

....

....

Continue on separate paper.

4 For this question, you need to refer to the **whole** of **Source B**, together with **Source A**, the account of the accident in the mine in Chile.

Compare how the two accounts convey their different attitudes to the mining disasters.

In your answer, you could:

- compare the different attitudes conveyed
- compare the methods they use to convey their attitudes
- support your ideas with references to both texts.

[16 marks]

....

....

....

....

....

....

....

....

....

....

....

....

....

....

....

....

....

....

....

Continue on separate paper.

Section B: Writing

5. 'Health and safety in schools and colleges or at work is not taken seriously enough. We need to do something about this urgently.'

Write a letter to your local member of parliament, arguing for or against this statement.

(24 marks for content and organisation

16 marks for technical accuracy)

[40 marks]

....

....

....

....

....

....

....

....

....

....

....

....

....

....

....

Continue on separate paper.

Practice papers for English Literature are available online. Visit: www.scholastic.co.uk/gcse

Answers

English Language

You should also refer to the mark schemes for AQA English Language when checking your answers.

Paper 1 Section A: Reading

Question 1

Do it! (page 16)

Things that suggest the Englishwoman is surprised or puzzled:

* Her 'face looked puzzled'.
* She seems surprised that Hortense's husband did not go to meet her.
* She frowns when Hortense uses unfamiliar language and says, 'What?'.
* She asks Hortense if the luggage on the pavement is hers.

Question 2

Work it! (page 18)

Just as the words chosen show misunderstanding and a sort of clash of cultures, the styles of speech and narrative also stress collision between the two women. Hortense tries to give herself authority by speaking in flowing, extended sentences. By contrast, the Englishwoman speaks in short, abrupt sentences: 'What?'; 'It's the size of the Isle of Wight'; 'Hang on here'. The narrative confirms this abruptness too: 'She then shut the door in my face' is factual and direct and complements the way the Englishwoman speaks.

Do it! (page 19)

Answers could explore:

* Hortense's over-formal vocabulary and grammar suggest she is feeling vulnerable and is trying to sound impressive and full of authority.
* The Englishwoman's informal speech suggests she feels relaxed and in control: 'It's', 'he's', 'Hang on'.
* Simple, short sentence, 'She then shut the door in my face', suggests Hortense is surprised/confused/offended.
* The Englishwoman's colourful hyperbole (exaggeration), 'It's the size of the Isle of Wight', suggests that the woman is feeling playful and humorous.

Do it! (page 20)

Answers could explore:

* The contrast in the two women's registers of language – Hortense is absurdly formal, the Englishwoman is very direct and informal.
* The Englishwoman's use of very direct, short questions.
* The 'white island' pun is used to draw attention to the two women's very different cultural backgrounds.
* Hortense's description of the woman's 'gentle giggle that played...', which tells us how much more relaxed the Englishwoman is than Hortense.

Question 3

Do it! (page 23)

Answers could explore:

* The clear and striking description of the Englishwoman at the beginning, so that we have this as a reference point for the rest of the episode.
* The use of dialogue rather than narrative to reveal the mutual misunderstandings of the two women, so that we share the confusion with Hortense.
* The contrasting patterns of language used by the two women.
* The role of the last paragraph in providing a sort of amazed commentary by Hortense, as she tries to account for her confusion.

Question 4

Do it! (page 26)

Answers could explore:

* To what extent *do* you agree? After all, Hortense's behaviour and confusion might be caused by her sense of vulnerability, so we could wonder if her behaviour is not typical of her.
* What impression of Hortense do you get? Is she a snob? Is she foolish to use language that she clearly cannot control? Is she over-concerned with appearances and with giving an impression of her 'superiority'?
* How do you feel about Hortense? What is your reaction to her? Do you feel sympathy for her?
* Look at some particular details in the text and ask yourself how these affect your reaction to Hortense. For example, explore the effect on you of her imagining that she will need 'ropes and pulleys to hoist me up'. The choice of 'hoist' creates an amusing mental picture.

Do it! (page 27)

Answers could explore:

* To what extent do you agree? Do you find yourself warming to her? If so, why?
* What impression of Hortense do you get? Do you think her mistakes make her look foolish?
* Look at some particular details in the text and ask yourself how these affect your reaction to Hortense.

Paper 1 Section B: Writing

Question type 1

Do it! questions (page 30)

Answers could include:

* A description of the whole scene, followed by a section of the scene, followed by one detail in that section – a sort of 'zooming in' approach.
* What is the mood or feeling of the scene? Try to capture/evoke that mood in words.

- Write in the present tense as though you are there and writing as you look.
- Are there any smells and sounds you could describe, as well as sights?

Question type 2

Do it! (page 32)

The answer could include:

- A lovely surprise, such as being taken to a football match or a theme park.
- Describe how you were feeling just before the surprise.
- Describe your reaction to the exciting thing.
- The use of some similes and metaphors to make your descriptions more original and fresh for the reader.

Do it! (page 32)

The answer could include:

- The difficult decision.
- Describe how you were feeling just before you had to make the decision. Worried, nervous?
- Describe how you were feeling after you had made the decision. Relieved or still worried?
- The use of some similes and metaphors to make your descriptions more original and fresh for the reader.

Question type 3

Do it! questions (pages 33–5)

Answers could:

- Start by setting the scene with an interesting description based on the picture.
- Write in the first person as the narrator describing the scene suggested by the picture.
- Start with a 'teaser' such as, 'As I looked out of my window that morning, how could I possibly have known that this was the last time I would see this familiar scene for a very long time?'
- Start the next section of the opening with someone or something coming into the scene from outside the picture.

Question type 4

Work it! (page 36)

At last Tessa was ready. She had planned carefully and in in secret. In some bushes at the edge of the cove, her boat was waiting for her, its oars stacked neatly. Supplies of food, water and essential equipment were neatly stored under the seats. In the moonlight her groping hands found the stern of the boat and she shoved hard. At first – weighed down with its cargo – the boat resisted her efforts, but suddenly with a scrunching noise the boat released from its hiding place and slid over the sand and into the water with a gentle whoosh. One last agonised push with her injured arm and the boat was floating. Joy pulsed through her body, driving out the pain, as she realised she was nearly free. But then worry nagged at her again: how long would she be on her own out at sea? How long could she survive? She still had no answer to these dreadful doubts.

Do it! (page 37)

The answer could include:

- What you were getting away from.
- What made you decide to get away when you did.
- Your feelings.
- How you prepared.
- The moment/day you got away.

Do it! (page 38)

The answer could include:

- What the dare was.
- How the dare came about.
- Why someone was tempted to do the dare.
- Start the story with the dare taking place, and then jump back in time.

Do it! (page 38)

The answer could include:

- What was unusual about the journey.
- Where you were going.
- Why you were going on the journey.
- How you got there.

Question type 5

Work it! (page 39)

... could feel his confidence draining out of him: he wasn't so jokey and carefree now. He too was overcome with dread about what might happen next.

Omran hated cobwebs and dark, damp places, but he pushed on until he was out of range of the others' whimpering and whining. He could see nothing now and so he stretched his hands forward and felt his way ahead. Occasionally he stumbled as – blind and terrified – he inched his way forward, and he had to reach into the menacing blackness to find something solid by which he could steady himself and stop himself from falling headlong into whatever his overheated imagination could summon up. Then he met something very real. Something solid. Something that there was no way through or around.

Do it! (page 40)

Answers could include:

- They are lost in a forest.
- They are in the forest because they dared each other to go deeply into the forest.
- One of them is injured.
- The situation allows them to learn things about themselves and each other.

Do it! (page 40)

Answers could include:

- What the misunderstanding was.
- Who the misunderstanding was between.
- What the consequences of the misunderstanding were.
- How the misunderstanding was resolved.

Paper 2 Section A: Reading

Question 1

Prepare it! (page 44)

- It is wise to plan carefully. We need to know that 'throwing caution to the wind' means being careless.

- Your safety and happiness will depend on good planning. We need to know that 'attention to detail' means *more than* just attention: it means doing something about it.

- Poor planning will lead to avoidable miseries. We need to realise that 'attention to detail' is another way of saying 'careful planning'.

Work it! (page 45)

A, D, E, H

Do it! (page 45)

B, C, G, H

Question 2

Prepare it! (page 46)

Tick:

Similarities

Preparations for sleeping outdoors

Do it! (page 47)

Answers could include:

- Shelter.
- Something to sleep in.
- Being unobtrusive.
- Carrying your sleeping equipment.

Do it! (page 48)

Some similarities:

- Both are light-hearted (at times).
- Both use informal (colloquial) phrases (e.g 'look into bivi-bags' in Source A; 'This child of my invention' in Source B) to suggest a slightly flippant, jokey attitude.
- Both use precise technical terms to convey authority.

Differences:

- Source A is encouraging and helpful; Source B is a narrative account and does not encourage readers in general to try wild camping.
- Source B suggests a more individual and amateur approach to wild camping – an approach based on improvisation and experiment.

Question 3

Prepare it! (page 49)

A and E are only about content.

Do it! (page 50)

Answers could include:

- Short, factual statements make Stevenson sound authoritative.

- Precisely described details suggest he knows what he is talking about: he is a confident expert.

- The use of the present tense in the early lines suggest that he is able to draw wise conclusions from a lot of personal experience: he is able to generalise from his experience.

- A teasing edge to Stevenson's tone suggests that he is not the fool we might assume he is: he is laughing at us for doubting him.

Do it! (page 51)

Answers should explore Stevenson's choice of language.

Question 4

Do it! (page 54)

Answers could include:

- Source A gives advice, whereas Source B gives an account of his own personal preparations with no attempt to convince readers that these were the best possible preparations.

- Although Source A does use humour, it is very practical and gives clear, professional advice. Source B maintains a personal, entertaining tone throughout, even though useful advice could be extracted from the account.

- Source B sounds as though wild camping must be a solitary activity and that avoiding company is one of its delights. Source A does not imply this, and does not overtly assume that a wild camper will be a solitary camper.

- Source B is clearly literary and rhetorical in tone, making use of a number of literary devices for effect. The main purpose of Source A – by contrast – is to give clear information and advice rather than to entertain.

Do it! (page 55)

Answers should compare the different attitudes of the two writers and compare the methods they use to convey those attitudes. References to both texts should be used to support ideas.

Paper 2 Section B: Writing

Work it! (page 59)

C (Band 4); A (Band 3); B (Band 2)

Work it! (page 60)

The right to vote was won in 1832, but even then very few people were included in the electorate: basically, you had to be rich to be allowed to vote. As time went on, more and more men were given the right to vote. By the end of the 19th century, almost every man had the vote. Women, however, had to wait until 1930 before they all got the vote on equal terms with men. Then, much later in the 20th century, the voting age was lowered from 21 to 18. It does seem that over time, the vote has been going down. In 1930 many people claimed it would cause chaos to give women below 30 the vote. In the 1970s many people claimed it would cause chaos to give the vote to eighteen-year-olds. But chaos did not follow. If we reduce the voting age again to 16, then the same sorts of people will predict chaos and the end of the world as we know it. History tells us that they will be wrong again.

Technical accuracy

Work it! (page 61)

The most important consideration is not how old a voter is, but how mature they are, some people are old and immature, while others are both young and very mature. Instead of giving anyone a vote when they reach a certain age, it might be wiser to give them a test first to find out how sensible they are. Some elderly voters might fail this test; they would have to give up their vote along with their driving licence. This rule might mean that the electorate would include some voters who are as young as 16, but some older people might become ex-voters.

Do it! (page 62)

Answers should take into account the required audience, subject matter, form and purpose.

Do it! (page 64)

Answers could include:

- A series of paragraphs, each containing one developed point, not too assertively presented.
- How life was/would be different without the internet.
- How a couple of specific examples of aspects of the internet have improved life.
- Possible bad effects of some aspects of the internet.

English Literature

Answers will vary according to the material studied. You should refer to the mark schemes for AQA English Literature when checking your answers.

Paper 1 Section A: Shakespeare

Work it! (page 71)

This is a well-organised and relevant response. Well-chosen references effectively support points made. The answer points out some ways Shakespeare's language affects the audience, although none of these are well-developed. Consideration of possible differences in audience reactions over time is useful. 'Emotive language' is correctly and usefully identified. To get into Band 5 the answer needs to more fully explore the effects of Shakespeare's language choices.

Paper 1 Section B: The 19th-century novel

Work it! (page 77)

Other points that could be explored include:

- Unnecessary repetition: e.g. 'breathless' is basically the same as 'can hardly keep up'.

- Many of the foods are described as though they are fat humans so that we get the connection between the foods and their potential to fill bellies that are often empty.
- Foods are sometimes described as though they are begging to be eaten – 'entreating', 'beseeching'
- The very long, 'rolling' sentences seem to envelop the reader as though they are inside the shops among all the ripe foods.

Paper 2 Section A: Modern texts

Work it! (page 84)

This is a thoughtful and generally well-organised response. Precisely chosen quotations are fluently integrated into the answer. The answer points out some ways the writer uses to manipulate the audience to be on the side of the inspector. The reference to the historical context is very relevant and adds to our understanding. 'Dramatic irony' is correctly and usefully pointed out. The answer would be even better if some of the writer's methods were explored more fully, with some analysis of their intended effect on the audience.

Paper 2 Section B: Poetry

Work it! (page 90)

This paragraph deals with the contrast between the mother and son very well, and it roots its analysis in relevant, well-chosen details from the text. Explanations use precise subject terminology which allows the student to make perceptive points quickly and efficiently. The use of hesitant language such as 'this *could* suggest...' and 'it's *as though*...' helps the student to interpret and consider possible explanations rather than treating the poem like something that has definite answers. The answer would be even better if the student occasionally paused and explored the nuances of particular features. For example, what does the word 'pinch' suggest that – say – 'hold' wouldn't? What is so 'endless' about the sky? Why did he choose to emphasise that feature of the sky?

Paper 2 Section C: Unseen poetry

Do it! (page 95)

Answers could include:

- The teacher does not trust the student, and is not sensitive to them.
- A very unequal relationship – no dialogue.
- The account is looking back (even though it is written in the present tense for immediacy), so there is a suggestion that the teacher is ashamed of how he treated the student.
- The unusual use of the word 'you' means that the whole narrative is in the second person. It sounds as though the poet is accusing the teacher, or as though the teacher is trying to distance himself from himself, referring to himself as 'you', not 'I'.

Do it! (page 97)

Answers could include:

- We are sorry for the students – especially because the teachers seem so insensitive.

- The way the teachers speak is harsh and very unkind (although in 'Your Dad Did What?' the teacher's words are only implied.)

- The second poem explores the development over time of the student's experience, whereas the first poem deals only with the experience itself – and its implied effect on the teacher.

- Both poems use rhyme to shape the narratives and give extra force to the lessons that we/the teachers/students should learn from the events.

Answers to the practice papers are available online. Visit: www.scholastic.co.uk/gcse